S0-ACA-438

& &

&

A

New

Treasury

Of

Sports

Humor

Prentice-Hall, Inc., Englewood Cliffs, N. J.

By

Herman L. Masin

Editor, SCHOLASTIC COACH

# A New Treasury Of Sports Humor

*A New Treasury of Sports Humor*
by Herman L. Masin

Library of Congress Catalog Card No.: 64-18622



PRINTED IN THE UNITED STATES OF AMERICA

61585—B C

& &

&

## Preface

As the most demonic sports anecdotist east of Duffy Daugherty, I'm frequently asked how I manage to keep dredging up so many pearls of wit year after year.

There's nothing to it, folks. All you need are a dozen magazine subscriptions, recourse to seven daily newspapers, access to three libraries, constant whirls around the fried chicken-and-peas circuit, a million joke-oriented buddies, a lot of guts, and a sharp pair of scissors. Then you're in business—if you want to call it a business. My compatriot, Bennett Cerf, does.

I started it, shortly after the storming of the Bastille, when I was compelled to take over the "Coaches' Corner" department in *Scholastic Coach*. And it has just "growed and growed" into six anthologies—the two largest being produced by the indulgent publishers of this volume.

The reason for my modest success is no more devious than that of *Playboy*. Everyone enjoys a good chuckle, but particularly the coach. I say "particularly," because the humorous anecdote has become more than an apertif for the coach. It has become part of his bread and butter. Whenever the coach steps up to address a school assembly, a Rotarian luncheon, a clinic, or an alumni group (may its tribe decrease), he's *expected* to warm 'em up with a funny story. This has become as traditional as the changing of the guards at Buckingham Palace or by Paul Brown.

Why the coach is expected to be funny, I knoweth not. But I wouldn't change it for the world. It would louse up a lucrative racket. Since the coach's stock of jokes is as vital to him as his playbook, game film, and bottle of tranquilizers, it stands to reason that a book of this nature fills a distinct need. It furnishes the coach with all the small arms he needs for his speech-making arsenal.

It's with this thought in mind—and my royalties, of course—that this anthology is casually presented. I had a helluva funny time putting it together, and I hope you have the same sort of time reading it and swiping from it.

& &

&

## Dedication

*I unjokingly dedicate this book to my six pillars of wisdom and philanthropy:*

AL DAVIS, Coach-General Manager, Oakland Raiders
CLIFF FAGAN, Secretary, National Federation
SID GILLMAN, Coach-General Manager, San Diego Chargers
FRANK RYAN, Field Events Coach, Yale University
BILL THOMPSON, Football Hobbyist Extraordinary
FRED WILT, a Gentleman Who's Always on the Right Track
And to
ELLEN-RUTH POMERANTZ, who loves me most and reads me least.

& &

&

# Contents

& &

&

# I. Cheermen Of The Boards

**TO HAVE AND TO HOLD**

Terry Dischinger, the thin man of the Baltimore Bullets, got involved in a pushing contest with Wilt Chamberlain. Terry lost his head momentarily and made a threatening gesture at Wilt. The alert ref quickly threw his arms around Terry.

Terry, taking a quick look over the ref's shoulder at Chamberlain, promptly screamed, "Don't hold me! Hold him!"

& &

&

**SHAGGY PYGMY STORY**

The goon center of the Pygmy Olympic Team was a shy kid who was very sensitive about his height. Every morning he'd look into the mirror and sigh:

*Mirror, mirror, on the wall,*
*Who's the tallest man of all?*
*With every player just 2-feet-7,*
*Why must I be 3-feet-11?*

**FOUL PLAY**

During the 1963 Holiday Festival at Madison Square Garden, a St. John's player screamed at Charley Eckman that he had been fouled. The colorful ref looked at the complainer disdainfully. "Young man," he said, "you gotta shoot better than that before you can officiate."

**THEM DRY BONES**

Bones McKinney is one of those perpetual emotion machines who keeps spewing a steady stream of advice to his kids on the floor. One night, an irate ref slapped a technical foul on Bones for coaching from the sideline.

The reporters turned toward Bones for the inevitable explosion. The Wake Forest coach surprised them. He sat back on the bench quietly, without even a grimace.

After the game, one of the writers cornered Bones in the locker room.

"Say, Bones," he queried, "you sure surprised us. How come you didn't object to that technical for coaching from the sidelines?"

"Young man," replied Bones loftily, "my coaching is worth a foul any time."

**SCHAYES LOUNGE**

Before the 76ers' first game against the *Celtics*, Coach Dolph Schayes was asked how he liked coaching in the NBA. The former star player smiled, "It's very interesting. But next year I'll take a psychology course on how to get along with officials. Maybe I'll copy Red Auerbach and give them all a box of cigars."

The *Celtics* nipped the 76ers that night, thanks to a dubious call in the last five seconds. After the game, Dolph was asked if he had changed his mind about giving the officials cigars.

"Yes," snapped Schayes. "I've now decided to give them cigarettes."

**TRAVELING TIME**

Eddie Conlin was the best player Coach Johnny Bach ever had at Fordham. A cleancut, dedicated, All-American boy, Eddie was drafted by the Syracuse *Nats*. In his first outing, he was assigned to the great Jack Twyman.

Right after the opening tap, Twyman took a pass in the corner. Conlin, the eager college kid, quickly moved in on him. Twyman feinted a drive, and Conlin properly took a step backward. Then, to Eddie's amazement, Twyman took *three* quick steps back and put up a shot. Swish!

The outraged Conlin turned to the ref, Sid Borgia. "Sid, Sid!" he cried. "The guy took *three* steps! Why didn't you call it?"

"Aw, c'mon, kid," replied Borgia, the hardened pro. "They were only *teeny weeny* steps."

**BACH TO NATURE**

Fordham was playing Duquesne in the finals of the Carousel Tournament. Behind 21 points late in the game, Coach Bach called for a press. Little by little the *Rams* whittled away the lead.

With about thirteen seconds to go, they tied the score, then stole the ball. Bach, elated, called time, and set up a play.

"Remember, boys," he warned as he sent them back onto the floor, "hold the ball for only one shot and be sure to make it a good one."

Fordham began passing the ball around and eventually it found its way into the center's hands. To Bach's horror, the boy started dribbling away from the basket, then, with seconds to go, he turned and took a wild hook shot from about forty feet out. The shot missed, Duquesne took the rebound, threw a long pass, and fired a desperation shot—that hit!

As Fordham plodded off the court, Bach cornered his center. "John," he moaned, "why, oh why did you ever take a shot like that after all I had told you?"

"Coach," the boy said loftily, "sometimes you have to be dashing and daring in this game of basketball."

### PLANE AND SIMPLE

When Connie Dierking broke in with the *Nats*, he had a phobia about flying. He simply couldn't get aboard a plane. Coach Paul Seymour approached his big center, Johnny Kerr.

"Johnny," he said, "you've been around a lot, You're not afraid of anything. The fellows respect you. Will you try to talk Connie out of his crazy fear of flying?"

"Sure, Coach," replied Kerr. He took Dierking aside and began telling him how foolish he was, how safe flying really is, that millions of people take planes every day, that accidents are rare.

"Besides," he concluded, "even the railroads have accidents. Did you read about the big accident in the Midwest the other day? Six cars fell off the track, killing 11 people."

"Gee," said Dierking, impressed, "how did that happen?"

"Oh," said Kerr, "a jet plane with 77 passengers fell on it."

**THE KID FROM BIG D**

Talking about the great high school players of the past season, Coach Red McManus of Creighton was lamenting his inability to recruit one of the truly great stars.

"I looked up his transcript," he groaned, "and the kid was so dumb he got a D in lunch."

**PASSING THOUGHT**

Over lunch one afternoon, Al Bianchi, the Philadelphia backcourt man, called to Dolph Schayes at the next table:

"Hey, Dolph, shoot me the ketchup."

Schayes obliged, then turned to a sportswriter next to him. "See?" he grinned, "they know I'm a shooter, not a passer."

**CUT DOWN TO SIZE**

Needing a suit of clothes, 6–9 Johnny Kerr, Philadelphia veteran center, went to visit his favorite tailor. The tailor carefully measured him for the suit plus an extra pair of pants.

Kerr then explained that he was going on a long road trip, and that he'd appreciate it if the tailor gave him the material so that he could have the suit made in Boston. The tailor acquiesced.

Upon reaching Boston, the big redhead got the address of a good tailor and deposited the material, telling the man he'd pick up the suit on the return trip.

About ten days later Kerr arrived, accepted the completed suit, and went into a booth to try it on. To his amazement, he discovered that the coat sleeves came up to the elbows and that the pants came down only to his knees.

Indignant, he strode out to the tailor. "Look, mister," he snapped, "back in Philadelphia, my tailor, a good man, gave me enough material to make up a full suit with two pairs of pants. Now look at the fitting of this suit!"

The tailor looked at pants, nothing more than Bermuda shorts, and the short coat.

"Buddy," he said softly, "all I can say is that you must be a bigger man in Philadelphia than you are in Boston."

**GENTLEMAN'S AGREEMENT**

Having signed to coach Boston College in 1963–64, Bob Cousy decided to take a day off from the Boston *Celtics* to size up his future squad. A varsity-freshman scrimmage was scheduled for that afternoon, and Bob volunteered to play with the frosh.

A few minutes after the tap, the Cooz intercepted a pass. Down the court streaked the fabulous young *Eagle*, John Austin.

"Mr. Cousy, Mr. Cousy," he yelled, "I'm open!" Everyone dissolved into laughter.

Frank Power, the interim coach, beckoned to young Austin. "John," he said, "this proves two things. First, you're smart enough to call for the ball when you're open, and two, you're a gentleman."

**THAT'S STALL, BROTHER**

A hook shot from Buzzy Lambert, hoop coach at Francis Scott Key High School, Union Bridge, Maryland:

"In a game between our Scott Key *Eagles* and Mt. Airy, we were playing a possession game with the score only 12–9 in the third period. We had been freezing the ball for over seven minutes, so naturally all the action was at one end of the floor.

"During the stall, one of our young substitutes, David Zentz, somewhat impatient with the lack of action, leaned over to me and pleaded, 'Coach, can we have a couple of balls and go out there and shoot at the basket that's not being used?' "

**CARNEVALE TIME**

When the ebullient King Kong (Red) Klein was starring for the great NYU basketball teams of the mid-thirties, he was approached one afternoon by his coach, Howard Cann, who had a tall, handsome, bashful youth in tow.

"Red," said Howard, "you know Ben Carnevale. He's just matriculated at NYU and is quite a ball player. Since he comes from your home town, I'd like him to room with you at the varsity house. Be a buddy and take good care of him."

"Don't worry, Howard, I'll take good care of him," promised Red.

"And I did take good care of him," Red will tell you now. "The next night I took him to Jersey City to play pro ball under an assumed name."

**TIMER ON THEIR HANDS**

The head basketball coach took his assistant on a fishing trip way up in Manitoba. The only other person at camp was an ugly old squaw, who had been hired by the day by the head coach. After watching the old squaw sitting around doing nothing for nine days, the assistant approached his boss.

"Coach," he inquired, "why did you ever hire that old ugly squaw?"

"Oh, she's the time-keeper," answered the coach.

"What do you mean, 'time-keeper'?"

"Well," explained the coach, "when that ugly old squaw starts looking good, it's time to go home."

**NOT TO QUESTION WHY**

Two questions put Michigan's star, Bob Cantrell, out of the Indiana game. Cantrell was hit accidentally on the chin late in the first half, but waved Coach Strack and the trainer away, shouting, "I'm all right."

In the lockerroom, Strack asked Cantrell if he felt okay.

"Sure," replied the player, "but can I speak to you privately?" They retired to a corner, and Cantrell said:

"Two questions: Where am I, and who the devil are you?"

**HE HITS THE SPOT**

When Bill Boelter was coaching Drake, he handed several balls to his players and told them to practice shooting from the spots where they might expect to be shooting in the game.

The No. 12 substitute immediately took a seat on the bench and started arching the ball toward the basket.

**BLOCKED KICK**

George Wilson, the Detroit *Lions* coach, became a basketball buff one winter. His son played for the local high school, and George was always around to lend vocal encouragement.

One night the kid ran into foul trouble. Twice he was called for charging, and eventually he picked up his fifth foul, putting him out of the game.

In characteristic parental dudgeon, Big George tore into the official after the game.

"Mister," roared the *Lions* coach, "you certainly don't know the difference between charging and blocking."

The ref gave him a withering look.

"Mr. Wilson," he drawled, "if you know so much about blocking, why can't you teach it to your football players?"

### SLIPS THAT PASS IN THE NIGHT

One night several years ago, Bill Sharman, the shootingest backcourt man in the NBA, found himself in an unaccustomed position—under his own basket. He promptly uncorked a 78-foot pass to teammate Bob Cousy, standing under the offensive basket. To everyone's stunned astonishment, the ball swished right through the basket.

Cousy looked up and sighed. "Sharm," he observed, "never was much of a playmaker."

### HIS MARK IN THE WORLD

Coaching a junior high school five is often a tedious task, but there are always chuckles along the way.

One afternoon Harding Junior High (Lakewood, Ohio) found itself involved in a real rough contest. Leading by a point at the half, they returned to the lockerroom.

Coach David Starrett asked his stringbean center how he felt out there. "It's really tough, Coach," he answered. "Those guys are sure throwing around a lot of elbows."

Attempting to fire him up a little, Coach Starrett told him, "Well, just what do you think you're going to get when you get up to high school?"

"Straight A's, Coach," the boy quickly replied.

**BABY TRICKS**

Lay-up from Jesse Bedwell, basketball coach at Nasson College in Springvale, Maine.

"Watching me diagram plays on a blackboard at home, my little girl Sherry, a third grader, decided to get a blackboard of her own. The first day I inspected her handiwork and saw that she had drawn twelve X's and four O's, the X's being my team.

" 'Sherry,' I said, 'that's not right. You have too many X's.'

"Sherry looked at me with loving eyes. 'Of course, Daddy,' she replied, 'you want to win, don't you?' "

**CAUGHT ON THE REBOUND**

The California five was mighty proud of its defense under Pete Newell, the greatest defensive mentor in modern hoop history—until, of course, the 1960 NCAA final, when Ohio State hit sixteen of its first seventeen shots and missed only three during the entire half.

Gathering his demoralized kids around him in the lockerroom, Newell patiently explained that they'd have to get more board control.

"Darrell," he said, pointing a finger at his big All-America center, "we've got to get more rebounds off the defensive board."

"Gee, Coach," groaned the big fellow, "every ball I rebound has already gone through the hoop."

**PRIVY TO STATE SECRETS**

Upon learning that his star forward had failed a history course, the basketball coach called in the history professor for an explanation.

"Well," said the prof, "the only question I asked him on the final test was: 'Why did the pioneers go into the forest?' From an academic standpoint his answer was 100 per cent wrong, but from a sanitation standpoint it would have been 100 per cent correct."

**IMMOVABLE OBJECTS**

John Kerr, the big, red-headed wit of the Syracuse *Nats,* rebelled when his coach, Alex Hannum, told him to take up isometric contraction exercises.

"Alex," Kerr said, "I've been pressing against immovable objects for the last nine years—Mikan, Foust, Lovellette, Chamberlain, and Russell—and, believe me, it doesn't work."

**IN SOLITARY**

A few years ago, when quiz programs were the rage, the Mexico, Missouri, High quintet was leading Jefferson City by six points, going into the last three minutes.

During a time-out, Coach Gary Filbert told his boys

to go into their stall game. He warned the boy being guarded by Jeff City's good defensive man not to get into the pattern but to stay on the weakside away from the ball—keeping the defensive star with him.

The boy carried out his orders perfectly, and the two boys whiled away the closing minutes all by themselves near a sideline.

Just before the game ended, the Mexico boy turned to the Jeff City guard and, with a grin, explained, "Buddy, you're in the Isolation Booth."

**HITS**
**FOR HIS AVERAGE**

One of those New York City basketball phenoms who wound up at a big Midwestern college—despite a 95 IQ and a below-par academic average—returned for a short visit and was interviewed by a local sportswriter.

In reply to a question of how he was doing, he said:

"Great! We have a terrific freshman team and I'm playing the backcourt, averaging about 18 a game."

"How are you doing with the books?" inquired the sportswriter.

"I'm doing great!" he enthused. "I've got a 1.8 average, and all I need is 2.0 to be eligible."

**THE SON**
**ALSO RISES**

Matt Guekas, Jr., the 6–5 son of the former St. Joseph's star pivot man, decided to go to Miami rather than to his father's alma mater.

"How come your boy didn't go where you went?" a reporter asked Guekas Sr., now a Philadelphia radio announcer.

"I didn't go where my father went, either," Matt replied. "He worked in a mill."

**NO-FOUL RULE**

Pro basketball was a rough sport back in the days of the original *Celtics*. One night one of the *Celtics* got an elbow in the face, then a blow in the gut. He fell to the floor like a stricken ox.

Dave McMillan screamed "Foul! Foul!" at the official, but the official ignored him. When Dave kept yelling "Foul!" at him, the ref finally turned around.

"What do you mean, foul?" he bellowed. "His shoulders didn't touch the floor, did they?"

**SNAKE-PIT BAIT**

Driving to Atlanta for a game against Georgia Tech, Adolph Rupp stopped at a gas station for some refueling. He noticed a strange figure shooting an imaginary basketball at an imaginary basket.

"What's that guy doing?" the Kentucky coach asked the attendant.

"Oh, he used to be our high school coach. Don't pay any attention to him, he's slightly off his rocker."

"Tell him to keep on shooting," replied Rupp. "If we lose this game to Tech I'll be back to guard him."

**HOMER ON THE RANGE**

When Piggie Lambert coached at Purdue, he frequently used Shorty Ray as an official. They had been buddies for twenty years, but during a Michigan game Piggie started yelling, "Shorty, you're a homer!" The Purdue bench promptly began chanting, "You're a homer, Shorty."

The referee ignored coach and players until the next time he passed the Purdue bench. Then he snarled:

"Piggie, you must be a helluva coach if it took you twenty years to find out I was a homer!"

**REF SLEDDING**

Basketball has come a long way since Dr. Naismith nailed a couple of peach baskets to the balcony of his Springfield YMCA gym. But the "homer" still plies his nefarious trade. Johnny Bach, the Fordham coach, has had some unpleasant experiences with the species, and his favorite story concerns the eastern coach who brought his team to a midwestern college where it was deemed almost impossible for a visiting team to win.

The lights were bad, and late in a wild game the visiting coach called time and called over an official.

"I can't see the scoreboard," he said. "How much time is left to play and what's the score?"

"There's just one minute left to play," the ref replied, "and we're ahead by four points."

**POINTS**
**PRO AND CON**

When Clyde Lovellette scored his 10,000th pro point, it passed uncelebrated as far as the public was concerned. But the *Hawks* had a trophy ready for him in the lockerroom. Coach Paul Seymour made the presentation.

"Here it is, Clyde," he said, "a trophy commemorating your 25,000 points—the 10,000 you scored, and the 15,000 you gave up."

**A BAYLOR OF HAY**

To stir up the publicity mills one summer, Ben Kerner, the man who fires all those coaches in St. Louis, offered the Los Angeles *Lakers* $500,000 for Elgin Baylor.

This made his latest coach gasp:

"When I heard Kerner was offering a half-million dollars for Baylor, I thought he meant Baylor University."

**A DREAM WALKING**

The basketball coach ran into his assistant on the way to the gym and immediately started babbling:

"Oh, boy, did I have the greatest dream last night. I dreamt I met a beautiful blonde with a 38–22–38 figure, who grabbed me by the arm, told me she'd always admired me, then insisted upon taking me up to her room—where she introduced me to her 7–3 kid brother."

**LAST RIGHTS**

Pat Kennedy, the most colorful basketball ref of all time, was working a Rochester-Fort Wayne game, when a *Royal* player was fouled going in for a lay-up. Unfortunately, Pat's whistle got stuck in his throat. As he lay on the floor convulsed in agony, Rochester coach Les Harrison ran over, fell to his knees over the gasping ref, and cried:

"Pat! Pat! Before you pass out, motion that the basket counts!"

**TALKING TURKEY**

When Jim McGregor, the international basketball coach, arrived in Turkey to coach the national team, he found the country under martial law. All meetings of more than three people were forbidden, and curfew was 10:00 P.M.

"I had no problems with discipline," Jim will tell you. "And with a 10 o'clock curfew, I had 'em in great condition. My only trouble was we couldn't practice."

**ANXIOUS MOMENT**

The coach put the eager, young substitute into the ball game early in the fourth quarter, and the kid went wild. He sank six long shots in a row, pulling his team ahead after it had trailed by 10 points. He then called time and ran over to the bench.

"Coach," he asked anxiously, "do you think I'm shooting too much?"

**LOSING THE LEEDE**

The Boston *Celtics* were playing a big game one night, and Coach Doggie Julian was trying to figure the right substitution.

He had Ed Leede kneel before him, and talked to him for a while. Then he called another player, and still another.

With the three men now in front of him, Julian finally put the third man into the game.

On the way back to his seat on the bench, Leede turned to the crowd, raised both arms overhead, and said with a big grin:

"Many are called but few are chosen."

**GOT HIS NUMBER**

The *Celtics'* program used to carry lucky numbers, for which prizes were awarded to the holders. One of Doggie Julian's teams was once having trouble with George Mikan and, in a moment of pique, Doggie flung his rolled-up program away.

A fan promptly yelled: "Better keep it, Doggie! You might win the radio!"

**KEEPING IT CASUAL**

Matty Begovich, after a brilliant career in college and pro ball, turned to officiating and made a great ref for twenty-five years. Cool, sensible, witty, he never let a game get out of hand.

One day Penn started pressing Dartmouth in the closing moments, and the *Indians'* coach, Doggie Julian, became incensed. He thought the *Quakers* were deliberately fouling.

After an apparently flagrant foul, Doggie yelled to Matty: "Matty! That was a deliberate foul! Two shots!"

Begovich turned to the bench and shook his head. "Just a casual foul, Doggie, just a casual foul."

**RUSSELL OF SPRING**

About the only man who can do a halfway decent job on Wilt Chamberlain is the great *Celtic* center, Bill Russell. He explains it this way:

"Wilt is a special problem. He can do just about everything. So you've got to experiment from game to game and minute to minute. I use a three-part defense against him. One, I try to keep him away from the ball. Two, if that doesn't work, I try to stay between him and the basket."

Bill will pause at this point, and the observer will invariably ask, "And what's three?"

"Three," Bill will say with a grin, "is when everything else fails—I panic."

**FOUST IN WAR,
FOUST IN PEACE**

Larry Foust, *Piston* center, and Andy Johnson, tough *Packer* forward, got involved in a pushing contest one night. The refs finally tore them apart and restored order.

In the lockerroom afterward, Foust was boasting to Don Ohl, "Only one thing kept me from tearing that guy apart."

"What's that?" inquired Ohl.

"Fear," replied Foust.

**CONCERTO FOR COMB**

When the Texas and Texas *A & M* basketball teams became embroiled in a wild fist-fight one evening, Shelby Metcalfe, the *Aggies'* assistant coach, helped restore law and order. He says:

"I just got out my pocket comb and helped the Texas band play *The Star-Spangled Banner.*"

**PASS-IVE
RESISTANCE**

Tommy Heinsohn, the *Celtic* gunner, was fouled on the way up with the ball. The ref blew his whistle and yelled, "One shot."

"*One* shot!" howled Heinsohn. "What do you mean, one shot?"

"You weren't shooting," said the ref. "You were passing off."

"You're crazy!" snapped Tommy. "Everybody in the league knows I *never* pass off."

**WRIST ACTION**

The 1961–62 season was a tough one for the New York *Knickerbockers*. Even their trainer, Don Friederichs, came up with an injury. He pulled a tendon in his wrist while bowling.

"Don," said Coach Eddie Donovan with mock seriousness, "I never knew you'd contract the occupational pro basketball disease—unwillingness to give up the ball."

**AFTER THE BALL**

One of the high spots of the 1961 All-Star Pro Basketball Game was a dance contest featuring the twist. Three players—Willie Naulls, Oscar Robertson, and Walt Bellamy—entered it, with Bellamy emerging the victor.

"Well, Willie," said Richie Guerin after it was all over, "no one can ever again claim that you don't move without the ball."

**COUNTS–DOWN**

Mel Counts, the seven-foot soph center, put Oregon State into the 1962 NCAA championships, so you can't blame Coach Steve Belko for being so high on him.

"He's so good," raves Steve, "that you could cut him in two and he'd make a pair of darned good guards."

**DOUBLED-UP PLAY**

"You have to be on guard all the time in pro ball," declares Dolph Schayes.

"Like when I'm playing against the *Celtics* and Jim Loscutoff is taking me. He has a way of wearing you down. When I step back and take my set shot, the referee has his eye on me and everything is fine. Then the ball goes up and the referee follows it. That's when Jim goes into action. He bangs me in the stomach with his finger, and nobody sees it.

"There's only one way to prevent it, but it's a tough way—you have to shoot doubled up."

**GUARD ALMIGHTY**

The basketball coaches at Lower Adams High School, New Oxford, Pennsylvania, are very defense-conscious, and drill their boys hard on it right from the start of the season.

The morning after the first basketball practice, Mike Hall, a jayvee guard, was asked how he felt. Mike exclaimed:

"Man, I hopped out of bed this morning in a defensive position!"

**SAFE ALL AROUND**

The safest coaching job in sports would have to be Red Auerbach's. He's safe if the *Celtics* win, and he's even safer if they lose.

How come?

Because, as one sportswriter puts it, it would take a genius to lose with that sort of material. And even in pro basketball, nobody fires a genius!

**PLAYING IT COUSY**

Bob Cousy put on a spectacular show in a *Celtics-Hawks* championship playoff—until, with two minutes to go, a chest congestion choked him up.

Gasping for breath, his chest heaving, Cousy signalled the bench to take him out. The crowd rose and gave him a thunderous ovation.

"Listen to that ovation," murmured Tom Sanders to Cousy, sprawled on the bench.

"Ovation, hell," groaned the Cooz. "It's a eulogy. They think I'm going to die."

**POETRY CORNERED**

In his early years as a college coach, Frank McGuire had a great respect for Frank Keaney, the old Rhode Island State coach. Keaney used to inspire his boys with poetry, and it's said that his players started cutting and shooting before they left the dressing room.

McGuire decided that poetry must be the answer to inspired performance. Before his next big game, he gathered his St. John's team around him and began impaling them with several yards of Kipling, Benêt, Lindsay, and Whittier.

The boys appeared profoundly impressed. As they filed out of the dressing room, McGuire leaned back, flushed and happy—just in time to hear one of his stars exclaim:

"Gosh, fellers, we've *got* to win this one for Frank—he's gone nuts."

**GREAT DAZE FOR THE IRISH**

Before the 1962 NIT quarter-final playoff between Holy Cross and St. John's, the *Crusaders'* pep squad walked around the court carrying two huge, colorful signs.

One sign read:

FOLEY-O'CONNOR-KELLEY-MC CLORY-SLATTERY

The other read:

PALACE-CANAVAN-GALLAGHER-JORDAN-FOLEY

Following them closely was a group carrying a third sign:

WALL-TO-WALL IRISHMEN

**TARDY REJOINDER**

Kansas State coach Jack Gardner has always been a stickler for promptness.

Perhaps the biggest headache he ever had was Jim Rhead. Though a hard-working, dependable player, Jim was so active in extracurricular activities that he'd often show up late for practice.

One day he came a little late for an important workout, and Coach Gardner really blew his top. After bawling him out for five minutes, he said, "Well, Jim, what's the excuse this time?"

"Gee, Coach," replied Rhead in an injured voice, "this is the earliest I've ever come late."

## THE PRIVATE WORLD OF A WHISTLE TOTER

*By Hoyt N. Sandlin*

There must be an easier way to supplement a teacher's salary than officiating in athletics.

At least that's what I keep telling myself. But just when I'm about to be convinced of the advisability of selling insurance or punching tickets at the local drive-in movie, along comes the first crisp, fall night when the lights suddenly go on down at the stadium and the crowd starts gathering and I can hear the whistles blowing.

Then I know I'm sunk for another year. It must be the sound of those whistles blowing—like every true son of Whistler's Mother, I respond like a ricochet.

I start boning up on the rules book, attend the first rules meeting of the season, check the cleats on my football shoes, and break the news as tactfully as I can to my wife that she's got to start ironing those referee pants again.

And for what?

So I'll be the most unpopular man in the county? So I can tear up the feed line on my car twenty miles from town with thirty minutes left until game time? So I can drive through duck-drowning rains or on glassy pavements? So I can spend the next six months appeasing my wife and kids for my nights out?

Then there's always the night to look forward to—the night the athletic director pays you off with a muttered, "You weren't so hot in there tonight, son."

Or the night your wife sits next to the home team coach's wife and decides to tell her in a few choice words where *she* can go—the destination being roughly the same as the one where the coach's wife has been verbally sending *you* all evening.

Then you can look forward to calling three basketball games alone some night in a pint-sized gym where you can run off five pounds trying to be some place where ten other tennis-shoed individuals aren't.

But now that the fever's hit me again, I've got

to study the latest rule books, interpretation meeting folders or handbooks, case books, and the state athletic bulletin. Also, I can rearrange my family's schedule so I can attend all rules interpretation meetings and clinics within a fifty-mile radius, and all the local officials' group meetings. To say nothing of every other game in town—to check the other officials' techniques, of course.

I can study for and take the annual state rules exams. I can pay my registration fee, qualify for state membership, and get my new Official's card. Then I can start filling up my schedule.

I can replace my old shirt with a new long-sleeved knit one. (My wife is very understanding about these little expenses. She should be. I turn the checks over to her.)

And I can start exercising so I'll be able to run down the 100-yard field the first night without falling flat on my face.

Then I'm ready to start to my first game.

Do you know what the written law is requiring the fulfillment of contracts by athletic officials?

Well, sir, it's a mighty fine and fair ruling—if you happen to be looking at it from a coach's viewpoint, that is.

An official is excused from his obligation—that is, to show up for a game—under the following two conditions. I quote:

1. Death or severe illness of himself or of his immediate family.

2. Fire, flood, impassable roads, or other adverse acts of Providence.

Well, now, I think No. 1 demonstrates some very generous thinking—especially in view of it occurring to the official himself.

But now let's see. Suppose my wife has a baby. According to the medical profession, that doesn't fall strictly under "illness." It certainly isn't due to fire, flood, or impassable roads. I suppose, if the hiring coach was of a reasoning type of mind, it would be classified as "adverse act of Providence."

You might possibly get by in case of a tornado.

But suppose your brother came in from four years in Alaska, with only one night to spend: do you suppose the ruling accounts for that? Or for when the superintendent of the school where you're presumably a teacher, calls a faculty meeting for that night?

And I can't find a thing to cover the event of having been given two free tickets to the Oklahoma-Texas game last year, provided we could leave on Friday afternoon.

That's what I kept telling my wife. And telling her. And telling her. Did you ever try to reason with a wife who's frantically waving two free tickets before your dazed eyes and pleading passionately with you to "Just this once, let's go!"?

It can't be done. Let me tell you.

Like the seasoned Broadway stars, an athletic official knows that, no matter what the heartbreak, no matter what the cost, the show must go on. (That bit of overplayed drama didn't convince her either. It was six days before she spoke a word to me beyond, "Pass the bread" and "Your daughter just spilled her plate of spaghetti on the floor.")

But then, supposing that fire, flood, and the rest haven't occurred and it's even a fairly presentable night and the car has worked fine and you got to the game an hour ahead of schedule.

You've called the game with a minimum amount

of incompetent scorers and timekeepers, irate parents, late starting time, poor parking facilities, and sideline coaching.

Now it's all over and the coaches are muttering to themselves and the crowd is howling to itself. You can now slip away, along with the other officials, to the school dressing room for a good, hot, relaxing shower.

Have you looked real closely, lately, at a school dressing room? Well, it isn't exactly the Ritz. Or even the City Hotel or Ye Olde English Inne.

It's a slate-colored, concrete cubicle, ankle-deep in water, with the enticing aroma of dirty underwear and sweat-soaked teenagers. If you're unlucky enough to be bathing with the defeated team, it's steaming with a certain tense, constrained atmosphere of unshed tears and unspoken epithets.

It's a place to lose your left sock and your billfold and your ego. It has slippery floors and one towel rack. It's a fitting climax to your evening.

*So who wants to sell insurance?*

**11.**

**". . . 8,**

**9,**

**10,**

**And OUCH!"**

**HOME BREAKERS**

"Hey, Butch," cried the first burglar, "let's get outta here. We've broken into the home of Floyd Patterson."

"Oh, don't worry, pal," retorted his partner in crime. "Patterson won't fight for anything less than $300,000."

**PRIDE AND PREJUDICE**

"Just think," exclaimed the conceited ham-and-egg fighter, "millions of people will watch me

& &

&

fight on television, all over the country tomorrow night."

"That's right," snapped a boxing scribe, "and they'll all know the result at least ten seconds before you will."

**SOUR-CASM**

"What did you think of that big fight between Patterson and Liston, Mike?"

"Big fight! Why, if my wife and I had a fight like that, the kids would boo us."

**TWO C'S WORTH OF FAITH**

Back in the good old days of boxing, Vic Marsillo owned a gym in Jersey City. One day he received a call from a nearby Jewish Center: could Marsillo provide a Jewish fighter for a main-eventer at its annual smoker?

Of course, assured Marsillo—not in the least disturbed that he didn't have any Jewish fighters. He singled out his favorite gym fighter and told him, "Your name is now Louis Greenberg."

"But it's really Tony Minucci," the puzzled pug demurred.

"Not if you want to make $200."

So Minucci became Greenberg, was introduced as such from the ring of the Jewish Center, then went back to his corner, and, before answering the bell, knelt and crossed himself.

### POWERLESS OF POSITIVE THINKING

Little Junior came home the first day after moving to a new neighborhood and told his father, a young coach, "Dad, the boys around here are bigger than I am, and I think they're going to beat me."

His father was horrified. "Now that's not the right attitude son. You must think positively."

"Okay, Dad," the boy replied mournfully. "I'm *positive* they're gonna beat me."

### ON HIS HONOR

One of the more cynical boxing writers refers to a much-arrested former champion as a victim of circumstance. "Why, when he went to school he was an honor student—'Yes, your honor,' 'No, your honor.' "

**FLIES BY NIGHT**

While training for the Liston fight, Floyd Patterson was relaxing on a couch when a fly buzzed by. Quick as a flash, Patterson reached out and captured it.

"Not bad, Floyd," commented a veteran fight reporter. "But Young Griffo used to do it better 50 years ago. He used to win bets that he could catch flies with just his thumb and forefinger."

The champion's eyes twinkled. "It merely denotes progress," he said in his precise speech. "It proves that the flies are faster these days."

**INSULTING MISS**

Steve Belloise once fought a nonentity named Jean Stock in Paris. The Frenchman was such a wide-open target that Belloise's manager, Eddie Walker, whispered to his tiger between rounds:

"Steve, don't miss this guy or you'll insult him."

**LORD OF THE FLIES**

Not many people know that Frankie Frisch, the baseball Hall of Famer, once had boxing aspirations. One afternoon at the New York Athletic Club he got into the ring with the great old pro, Joe Welling, who promptly began jabbing his nose off.

When Frankie went berserk, Joe admonished him:

"C'mon now, stop going berserk every time you're tagged. Learn to pick off those punches. Just a flick of your glove will knock the jab aside. Pretend there's a fly on your nose and you're knocking it away."

Frankie tried to do what he was told, but it didn't work. He finally complained, "Joe, you're catching me in between flies!"

**GLOVE AND MARRIAGE**

Watching some of those awful boxing matches on TV, we're ready to believe the ancient adage that a prizefight is like marriage—the preliminaries are better than the main event.

**SMART PICKER**

Ribbed on his poor ability to pick fight winners, Jim Corbett replied:

"Let me tell you this. When I fought Jeffries at Coney Island, along about the third round I picked Jeffries to win."

**JACK IN THE PULPIT**

Beau Jack, the former lightweight champion, was a simple, gentle fellow who prayed before every fight. As he explained it, "I pray that nobody get hurt. Then I pray that it be a good fight."

"But don't you ever pray to win?" he was once asked.

"No," he replied. "Suppose I pray to win. The other boy, he pray to win, too. Then what's God gonna do?"

**MY MOM, THE ACCOUNTANT**

Even when the fighter became welterweight champion, his mother never stopped nagging him to quit.

"Now you're on top," she begged. "Quit before it's too late. Promise you'll stop fighting at the end of the year."

"But, Ma, you don't understand," protested the fighter. "I'm in the big money now that I'm champ. I'm likely to gross a hundred thousand dollars on my next bout."

"My boy," interrupted mama, "promise me you'll stop fighting in nine or ten years."

### TANKS FOR THE MEMORY

The 5-to-1 favorite had been bribed to take a dive in the fifth round. The underdog, secure in the knowledge that he couldn't lose, began bouncing left hooks off the favorite's chops.

"You dirty little double-crosser," hissed the latter in a clinch. "Just wait till I get you outside!"

### KING FOR A NIGHT

When Jack Dempsey ruled the heavyweights, he was always being accosted by aggressive drunks who wanted to boast they had taken a punch at the champ. The Manassa Mauler learned to handle them with grace—even when he was once awakened in the middle of the night by a hotel clerk.

"Sorry, Mr. Dempsey," apologized the poor fellow, "but there's a man down here in the lobby who says he can win your title, and he wants to have it out with you."

"That's all right, buddy," replied the champ. "Tell him he can have my title, but to bring it back to me in the morning."

### IN AT THE FINISH

At the wedding of a buddy, we happily found ourself

sitting next to an old friend, Les Bromberg, the crack boxing reporter. A highly articulate, intelligent, and witty gentleman, Les good-naturedly countered our violent diatribe against the slum of sports.

"Come on, Les," we finally smiled. "What are you going to cover after the fight game dies?"

"The burial, of course," Les drawled.

**POINT OF NO RETURN**

Dick DuBow, the terror of the Sixth Ward, took a terrific shellacking in his bout with the champ and finally took the full count in the third round. Coming to three hours later in his dressing room, he peered at his manager through the welts under and over his eyes and mumbled:

"Just get me a return match wid dat bum, Slippery, and you'll see a real massacre. I'll knock your block off."

**CATCHER IN THE WRY**

Told that he looks like Yogi Berra, Gene Fullmer, the former middleweight champ, remarked:

"I hope I can hit as well as Yogi, but I don't want to catch the way he does."

**A LIVING DOYLE**

When the marvelous Jack Doyle, the Hibernian heavyweight with the handspun glass chin, arrived in America in 1935, there was considerable controversy over his record. No one seemed to know exactly what it was. John Lardner, the famous *Newsweek* wit, took it upon himself to investigate, and this is the way he reported his findings:

> Your correspondent . . . has always taken a close interest in the Hibernian Thrush's career, and is glad to state the record officially. It is as follows:
> Fights 4.
> Marriages 2.

**THE BAER FACTS**

Lardner's description of the Jack Doyle–Buddy Baer fight is a classic:

> In the first round, Doyle feinted with his left and crossed his right to Baer's chin. He then stepped back to watch Buddy fall like a giant redwood tree, but Mr. Baer appeared not to have noticed the punch. His mind doubtless was on something else. He waved his hand at the man from Cork, who sank to the floor clutching his abdomen.
>
> The customers gathered from this gesture that Mr. Doyle believed he had been fouled. They could not bring themselves to agree with him and they uttered the Bronx salute so lustily that the victim, who had a quick ear for language, saw their point at once and got up. He hit Baer once more. Baer hit Doyle—and the Lark went down for five seconds.
>
> On rising he collapsed against the ropes, and the referee, Billy Cavanaugh, a Celt with strong national sympathies, stopped the fight.
>
> It was at this point that Mr. Doyle gave up prizefighting in America, where they took it too seriously, and devoted the remainder of his time among us

**to coeducation. His double career—boxing in England, marrying in America—came to an end soon afterward but before it did, he performed some of his most brilliant and unusual work in both fields.**

### SECRET TRAINING

"When Floyd Patterson was supposed to be holding secret training sessions the week before the Farce of the Ages," wrote Dan Parker, "everyone in his camp except his trainer and manager was barred. In view of what happened, maybe Floyd was practicing on a trampoline."

### A NIGHT AT THE HORSE OPERA

The folks who paid anywhere from $5 to $10 to watch this immortal smellodrama on pay TV must still be screaming, "Help! Police!" A delightful commentary on this was written by columnist Robert Sylvester:

> **Well, I seen the fight on pay TV all right. Six of us went to the RKO 86th St. Theatre and it only cost us $6.75 apiece . . . It was a good show, all right. The way it came out, this Lord Ambrose had stolen all the music from a poor young composer and this composer tried to burn up a printing plant and set himself on fire. He then became the phantom of the opera and caused everybody a lot of grief. There was considerable swimming back and forth in a sewer and at one point I went out and bought some RKO popcorn.**
>
> **They pour some grease on this stuff and it is delightful. For fight night it only cost 50¢ a pop. I went back and they were still swimming in that sewer but**

**by this time the whole mob in the theatre was rooting for the phantom.**

**Finally the phantom turned into a pretty square chap and got himself killed saving the girl. There was a lot of action in this theatre on fight night. After the phantom died they had a short subject from Chicago. This was about some other fight but they never did get the picture in focus so I dunno how it came out.**

### FROST ON THE PUMPKIN

"As a poet," writes Shirley Povich, "Cassius Clay may not compare with the late Robert Frost, but it may be true that he fights like him."

& &

&

# III. Tee-Hee Formation

## SPELLING BEE

After Notre Dame signed Ara Parseghian to a long-term contract, sportswriter Gordon Graham bumped into the Notre Dame publicity man, Charlie Callahan.

"Well, Charlie," teased Graham, "have you learned to spell it yet?"

"Sure," grinned Callahan. "It isn't so tough. It's P-a-r-s-e-g-h-i-a-n."

"I don't mean Parseghian," deadpanned Graham. "I mean Presbyterian."

& &

&

**PLATOON SYSTEM**

Before the 1964 Shrine Game, the East went through a long punting drill. Two guards, Michigan's Joe O'Donnell and Iowa's Mike Reilly, booted 'em a mile kicking left-footed. Another Iowan, Paul Krause, booted 'em a mile kicking right-footed.

"We're set for anything," declared Coach Jack Mollenkopf. "If the West throws a right-handed pitcher at us, we can send in a left-footed kicker."

**BOYS WILL BE BOYS**

Prior to the championship *Bears–Giants* playoff, Allie Sherman called a meeting of his *Giants* and, in the course of his talk, denied the then hot rumor that Del Shofner was to be traded for Paul Hornung.

"I wouldn't trade Del," emphasized the Giants coach, "for Hornung and all his girl friends."

"Now wait a minute, Coach," chimed a *Giant* lineman. "Don't you think we ought to take a vote on that?"

**MAMA'S BOY**

Hal Lebovitz, the Cleveland football official, once ejected a player for throwing a punch at an opponent. After the game, a large, wild-eyed man came barging into the dressing room demanding to know who threw the boy out.

"I did," Hal told him, preparing for the worst.

"That was my son," the intruder exploded. "Why'd you do it?"

Hal explained—the kid was having a bad day, missed some blocks, got trapped a few times, became frustrated, and began hollering and swinging.

The irate parent paused, red-faced but thoughtful, looked at Hal, and shook his head.

"Takes after his mother," he snapped, and stalked out of the room.

**WHAT COULD HAVE BEEN**

*Giant* fans are still moaning that if Del Shofner hadn't dropped an easy pass into the end zone in the second quarter of the *Giants–Bears* championship game, the *Giants* would have easily beaten the *Bears*. That would have made the score 14–0.

Much the same thing happened in that historic 1940 game in which the *Bears* beat the *Redskins*, 73–0. Early in the game, with the *Bears* leading only 7–0, a *Redskin* receiver also dropped a sure touchdown pass. Would the rout have been averted if the pass had been caught?

A reporter once asked Sammy Baugh that question. Sammy thought for a moment, then replied, "The score certainly would have been different. It would have been 73–6."

**HEAR**
**THE BRAIN WHISTLE**

The disgruntled head coach was discussing his staff with an old friend. "And then there's Pete Ottis, my line coach. He has the most unusual brain of all."

"That's bad?" queried the friend.

"It's this way," explained the coach. "Pete's brain starts working the moment he gets up in the morning and doesn't stop until he reaches the field."

**HEAD-LINER**

Nasty but real sharp is this observation by Dixon Ryan Fox:

"I listened to a football coach who spoke straight from the shoulder—at least I could detect no higher origin in anything he said."

**CANDID CAMERA**

The kid was walking down the street—more than a bit bruised, a little bloody, and completely bushed. "Are you a football player?" a kindly gentleman asked.

"No," the boy replied, "but I just left eleven fellows who are."

**NOBODY SECONDS THE MOTION**

Upon being appointed head coach of the *Giants* in 1961, Allie Sherman announced that he would restore the man-in-motion series to the *Giants'* attack. This prompted Kyle Rote to murmur, "Maybe we won't win many games, but we'll sure have at least one guy in great condition."

**A TURN**
**FOR THE BITTER**

Watching Notre Dame being buried alive by USC last fall, one of the *Fighting Irish's* nonacademic subway alumni mourned, "If Rockne were alive today he'd be turning over in his grave."

**SIRENE OF THE BRONX**

Fordham was running through its plays in its last workout before meeting Dr. Jock Sutherland's powerhouse Pittsburgh eleven. Tension was mounting and the *Rams'* coach, Sleepy Jim Crowley, searched for a way to break it. Suddenly the wail of fire engines rent the air. The players froze as the engines raced down the street in front of the campus.

"Don't be alarmed, men," said Sleepy Jim, "that's only the Pitt team walking through their plays."

**SHOCK THEATER**

Just before the kickoff, the rookie quarterback ran over to the sideline. "Coach," he panted, "what does it mean if you suddenly forget all your plays?"

**FINGER WAVES**

An attorney friend of ours, Myron DuBow, was trying to teach his five-year-old boy, Dick, how to catch a football. After one throw fell from his hands, the boy clutched his fingers and started yowling.

"Come on, Dick," the dismayed father reprimanded, "that couldn't have hurt very much."

"You did it on purpose, Daddy!" the boy shrilled accusingly. "You *aimed* at my fingers!"

**ROYAL EDICTS**

After surveying his 6-3, 260-pound freshman tackle, Coach Darrell Royal announced, "Jerry Oliver has the biggest hands and feet I've ever seen. We're going to X-ray his big toe. We think it has a liver in it."

And then there was this Royal crack about overweight players:

"Fat people don't offend me. What offends me is losing with fat people."

**SHIFTY WEAVER**

After being hanged in effigy, Kansas State coach Doug Weaver blandly remarked, "I'm glad it happened in front of the library. I've always emphasized scholarship."

**SCOUT'S HORROR**

When the *Giants'* coach, Allie Sherman, assigned one of his bird-dogs to scout the Green Bay *Packers,* he was surprised by the pained look that appeared on the fellow's face.

"What's wrong?" asked Allie.

"Coach," the fellow groaned, "how the hell do you scout blocking and tackling?"

**FLUNKIES**

While dressing after a tough scrimmage, three pro stars began discussing the circumstances that forced them to leave college to play for pay.

"I was a senior at Cornell," said the first, "and got grounded on calculus."

"It was advanced trigonometry that tripped me in my junior year at Stanford," chipped in the second.

The third player, late of Abnormal U., sat staring moodily into space. Then he spoke, "Say, did you boys ever run into a subject called long division?"

**COMMERCIAL AIR POWER**

The local high school coach cornered the sports editor of the town paper.

"Chuck," he gritted indignantly, "what am I going to do about those college recruiters? Do you know what one of them offered my star quarterback? Free tuition, room and board, $110 a month spending money, a month's vacation with pay, and a guaranteed lifetime job after graduation!"

"What college was that?" excitedly asked the sports editor.

"The Air Force Academy," grinned the coach.

**HEAVEN CAN'T WAIT**

A fine, outstanding athlete was killed in a freak accident; naturally, he went to Heaven. He conducted himself so magnificently for the next 100 years that Saint Peter sent for him and asked what the boy would like as a reward.

"Only one thing," the athlete replied. "My football letter."

Saint Peter assured him that the request was reasonable and that the boy would get it as soon as it arrived. The athlete waited 1,000 more years and then accosted Saint Peter. "Gosh," he said, "where's the letter you promised me?"

"My boy," said Saint Peter mournfully, "your letter arrived the day after you requested it. But we've been waiting these 1,000 years for a coach to show up and present it to you."

### IN A HAPPY HAYES

*Buckeye* fans are amused, maybe even a little proud, of Woody Hayes' renowned three-yards-and-a-cloud-of-dust offense. In the 1961 Iowa game, however, Ohio State kicked off and then couldn't get the ball back. Iowa kept moving the ball up the field, but was thwarted by penalties. A *Buckeye* lineman finally hit the Iowa quarterback, Matt Szykowny, from behind. The ball popped out of Matt's hands right into the mitts of an OSU end, who ran unmolested for a touchdown.

A wag in the pressbox crowed, "Well, you have to admit, Woody may have a stodgy offense, but he certainly opened up his defense."

### AGE OF REASON

The *49ers'* mastodon tackle, Leo Nomellini, was becoming increasingly annoyed at the elbows being thrown at him by the opposing tackle. Finally he rose to his full height, looked the fellow in the eye, and snapped:

"Look, Mr. 78, if you want to play rough, okay. But remember, you're pretty good-looking; me, I've got nothing to lose."

**ROUTINE PLAY**

Vince Lombardi was complimenting Dr. Norman Erdman on his marvelously cool, deft surgical technique. The good doctor shrugged off the accolade.

"Let me tell you something, Vince," he said. "For five years I worried before operations, the way you do before a game. But after you've done a hundred gastrectomies or a hundred colectomies it becomes almost routine. You almost always know where those organs are going to be. They don't keep shifting on you like a defense does, and they don't fight back."

**PROMOTING GENIUS**

Every NFL team passed up Ron VanderKelen in the draft. But after he riddled USC in the Rose Bowl, six clubs hastened to make offers. During the banquet circuit that winter, the *Trojans'* witty coach, Johnny McKay, explained it this way:

"Milt Bruhn, the Wisconsin coach, is a good man. But he had VanderKelen four years and all the kid got was a college scholarship. I had him for only four quarters and I got him $60,000!"

**NO PLACE LIKE HOME**

A friendly, warm, down-to-earth fellow, Johnny may be the only big-city, big-time coach whose home phone is listed in the directory. Anyone can call him at West Covina, Calif.

"It's mighty handy," explains Johnny. "When people tell me to drop dead, I can do it right on my own rug."

**BASKET CASE**

The New York *Titans* must have had little respect for their players' mental alertness during their 1962 summer camp exercises. Over a basket in their dressing room hung this sign:

THROW T-SHIRTS, SOCKS, AND
SHORTS IN THIS BASKET AND
PLEASE REMOVE THEM FROM YOUR BODY BEFORE THROWING

**IT'S A MAD, MAD, MAD WORLD**

Curious about the sudden disappearances of the head coach every afternoon, his assistants decided to tail him. He was found crouching behind a shrub near the local insane asylum, watching an inmate playing an imaginary football game. The inmate kicked an imaginary ball, ran to the other end to recover it, raced back to midfield and tackled himself. Then he'd run four plays on offense, change sides, and take four downs the other way. Finally he'd run to the goal line and throw up his hands to indicate a touchdown.

One of the assistants, amazed at all these shenanigans, walked over to the head coach and tapped him on the shoulder. "Good heavens, Doc," he said, "what in the world are you doing?"

"Look," said the head mentor, "the way our season is going I've gotta go nuts, and they're sure to shove me into this place and make me coach of one of their teams."

The coach's voice rose, "And if I don't scout this guy now, we'll get beat 50 to nothing!"

**MODELL BEHAVIOR**

In one of their first games under their new coaching setup, the *Browns* recovered a fumble and the offense team immediately rushed onto the field. Quarterback Frank Ryan bumped into defensive end Johnny Brewer coming off the field. Ryan whispered something into Johnny's ear, then Johnny continued to the sideline.

Up in the press box, Art Modell, the *Browns'* owner, promptly quipped: "How do you like that? We have a new messenger system—we're now sending plays to the BENCH!"

**IN THE NECK OF TIME**

In his football days at Michigan State, Sonny Grandelius was a human battering ram who could always get you those three yards when you needed them.

A haberdasher, looking at Sonny's massive head sunk low between his shoulders, once asked him, "What size neck do you have, sir?"

"I no longer have a neck," growled Sonny. "Too many of those darned third-and-one situations."

**QUICKEST DRAW IN THE WEST**

"I had this halfback," drawls Jack Curtice, "fastest starting back in Texas. So fast he was always drawing penalties for being in motion. One day I told the official to watch the boy closely and he'd see that the boy wasn't jumping the gun—he was just getting away like a jet.

"On the very next play the official penalized us again. I screamed that the boy wasn't in motion.

" 'No, he wasn't,' the official told me, 'this penalty is on the rest of the team for delaying the game.' "

**A LITTLE BIT FLAKEY**

The big tackle came running to the sideline, brandishing his helmet. "Coach," he complained, "one of the screws in the face mask has come loose." The coach calmed him down and showed him how the screw could be tightened with the buckle of the chin strap.

"That's pretty smart, coach," the boy said admiringly.

"Well," replied the coach, "after 20 years in the game I should have something under my hat besides gray hair."

"Coach," the boy grinned, "you're the first person I've ever heard say something nice about dandruff."

**JUST FOR THE HELL OF IT**

The *Heavenly Hot-Shots* and the *Satanic Swifties* were practicing for their big game for the championship of the universe. Every day they'd yell up and down to each other, bragging what one was going to do to the other. One day the jockeying got particularly sulphuric.

The *Heavenly* captain jeered, "We can't lose. We have all the All-Americans on our team."

The *Satanic* leader yelled, "So what? What are you guys going to use for coaches?"

**CLASS REUNION**

The deceased coach was greeted at the unpearly gate by Satan himself. "Buddy," said the Devil, "you were so terrible up on earth that we're going to give you VIP treatment. You have your choice of three rooms." The first room contained beautiful women; the second room contained wine and song; and the third room contained two dozen great coaches, who were standing on tiptoes in a cesspool right up to their chins.

The coach gaped, then exclaimed, "Good lord, this really is Hell!"

One of the fellows on tiptoes looked pained. "If you think this is hell," he gritted, "wait until the alumni come by in their motor boats!"

**STAR-GAZING**

The *College All-Stars* amazed the grid world in 1963 by defeating the supposedly invincible Green Bay *Packers*. It was a heck of a ball game, and one spectator, staggering out of Soldier's Field in a happy haze, exclaimed, "Gee, that one was so good I think I'll get season tickets!"

**PLEAS AND KARRAS**

After Emil Karras's astonishing confession about gambling on pro games, a cynical onlooker shook his head and muttered:

"One thing you have to say about Karras: no one can accuse him of not having the guts of his lack of conviction."

**HE MAKES YOU HOWELL**

After viewing our first Big Ten game—Ohio State vs. Iowa—we were invited to the biannual Sigh Youse fraternity banquet in Columbus, and what a ball we had! M-Ceeing the function was that priceless sportswriter and humorist Fritz Howell. He made the audience Howell at such nuggets as:

> **When I went to college, our team was so bad it had trouble making first downs against the wind. We had snake dances and victory banquets after winning the toss.**
>
> **Our fullback was All-American, but he was so dumb he won three letters before he could write one. He could do everything with a ball except autograph it. When he came late to practice one day, the coach told him to take one lap around the field. An hour later the coach discovered him still running.**
>
> **"Hey, Buster," the coach yelled, "what are you still running for?"**
>
> **"Coach," the monster groaned, "I lost count."**

### RISE OF THE GOLDBERGS

When Sleepy Jim Crowley was coaching Fordham and Harry Stuhldreher was coaching Wisconsin, the two charter members of the famous Four Horsemen had a mutual problem —how to stop Pittsburgh's great running back, Marshall Goldberg.

Before the Wisconsin-Pitt game one season, Stuhldreher and Crowley compared notes on the *Panthers.* Stuhldreher, who was given to wild dreams, told Crowley that he had experienced his worst nightmare.

"Marshall Goldberg had broken through our defense and was in the open racing for a score. In my nightmare I couldn't stand it any more. I leaped off the bench to tackle him. In reality, I sprang off my bed and hit the radiator. And that's how I got this black eye."

"Never mind the shiner," snapped Crowley. "Did you stop Goldberg?"

**GOAL LINE DEFENSE**

At a press meeting in Columbus, Bud Suter, the Iowa radio-TV public relations man, brought the house down with his recollection of his first trip to Columbus as a Drake halfback in 1935.

"We managed to tie the score at 7–7 in the first quarter, but instead of receiving Ohio State chose to kick off again. Our quarterback caught the ball, ran about 10 yards, then—to our astonishment—punted it. Tippy Dye took it on the goal line and raced 100 yards for a touchdown.

"We played the rest of the game between our one-yard line and our goal line. I played safety, and our tackles played right alongside me. The final score was 85-7."

**MUDDEN T OFFENSE**

Tom Nugent, Maryland coach, after a rain-soaked loss to North Carolina:

"It was so muddy that after I went out and congratulated the Carolina players, I discovered they were mine."

**THE VANISHING AMERICAN**

Though practically a midget, Eddie LeBaron has put in nine years with the big, tough pros. His height and weight seem to change from program to program, and a sportswriter finally put it to him squarely.

"Eddie," he asked, "exactly how tall are you, and exactly how much do you weigh?"

"Well," replied Eddie, "when I first started in the NFL, the program listed me as 5–9 and 175. After a while, that was changed to 5–8 and 170. Now I'm listed as 5–7 and 164. That must mean that over the years they've been cutting me down to my own size."

**STEPPED SHORT**

The fiery halfback blasted into the line and was knocked flat by a towering tackle. Disgusted and humiliated, he unloosed a string of oaths at his tackler. The referee stepped off 15 yards.

"What's that for?" stormed the irate halfback.

"For an illegal mouth," quietly responded the official.

**PACT DEFENSE**

Ron Mix, perhaps the greatest offensive lineman in pro football, and his coach, Sid Gillman, were locked in a bitter argument over Ron's contract. They finally came to a point where $1,000 separated them.

"Ron," the *Charger* coach-general manager said, "I have too much respect for you to quibble over $1,000."

"Coach," snapped Mix right back, "I have too much respect for $1,000 not to quibble."

**A QUICK MIX**

An astonishingly literate and articulate athlete, Ron Mix always worries about the man he'll be facing across the line every Sunday. Before he takes the field, he always utters the offensive lineman's prayer:

"May this unknown fellow be skinny, slow, weak, stupid, and love football but hate body contact."

**PASSING FANCY**

Joe Madro, the *Chargers'* line coach, is a craggy-faced perfectionist with a startling command of the language. His method of communication is a mish-mash of Jack E. Leonard, Aldous Huxley, and Henry Miller. One afternoon at the *Chargers'* camp, we were telling him about one of the most inept quarterback performances we had ever seen.

"This guy," we said, "kept over-throwing his targets, always managing to throw the ball over his receiver."

Joe nodded his head sagely. "Yep," he said, "some throw 'em to the birds and others throw 'em to the worms."

**STOOGE PIGEON**

Watching one of his linemen always raising up before going downfield, Joe Madro finally exploded:

"Plunkett, don't raise up so soon! You'll never get past those defensive men. You'll wind up looking like a statue. We'll then be able to stick you in a park and make all the pigeons with poor aim happy."

**BUCKING BRONKO**

One fall afternoon that rock of all ages, Bronko Nagurski, gave the Pittsburgh *Steelers* a dreadful beating. On the way home after the game, the *Steelers'* train came to a jolting halt, catapulting everyone into the aisles.

"Run for your lives, men," shouted an impish halfback. "That guy Nagurski is still after us!"

**WHEN THE BAUGH BREAKS**

In his later years with the *Redskins*, Sammy Baugh had to fight for his life every time he dropped back to pass. The blockers simply couldn't contain the rushers. Just before Sammy hung up his helmet for good, he was asked to take a bow at a gathering of FBI agents.

Sammy got to his feet, casually surveyed the G-men all around him, and drawled, "Gentlemen, this is the most protection I've had all year."

**THE MARSHALL PLAN**

Bosom buddies off the field but hateful enemies on it, George Halas and Preston Marshall made a colorful team in the early years of the NFL. One of their worst donnybrooks occurred right in front of the Marshall box before the shocked eyes (and ears) of Mrs. Marshall.

The old boys filled the air with purple language and finally had to be pried apart by the gendarmes. Preston found his wife with her hands over her ears.

"What horrible language!" she shuddered.

"You shouldn't have listened," Marshall said.

"As for that Halas," continued the Missus, "he's absolutely revolting." He's a—"

"Now wait a minute," interrupted Marshall. "Don't you dare talk about my best friend that way."

**ALIAS JIMMY VALENTINE**

Late one night at the *Giants'* training camp, coach Jim

Lee Howell heard a noise in the corridor. He stepped outside the door and surprised a defensive end tiptoeing down the hall with his shoes in his hand.

"You going somewhere?" asked Jim.

"Why, yes," the end said, exhibiting great reflexes, "I lost my wallet, so I thought I'd go out and try to find it."

"I see," said Jim, looking at the shoes. "You planning to sneak up on it?"

**WRONG KIND OF PULL**

In his days at Fordham, Jim Crowley drilled his guards endlessly on pulling out of the line. One afternoon in a dummy drill without helmets, Nat Pierce pulled left and Vince Lombardi pulled right. They met behind center like a head-on auto collision. Both fell to the ground stunned.

Crowley walked over, looked down, and said just one word: "Typical."

**'TAINT FUNNY, MC GEE**

On an option pass from his buddy Paul Hornung, Max McGee made a hair-raising one-handed catch in the end zone. After the game, a sportswriter asked Max about the catch.

"Hornung is supposed to make me look good on those," Max explained. "On that one, though, he made me look ridiculous."

**BEHIND IN HIS PRAISE**

The third-string right halfback broke inside the left guard for a 35-yard gain. As he reached the five-yard line, the safety man caught him from behind with a desperation tackle that pulled the halfback's pants down to his ankles.

The coach, from the sidelines, hollered. "Great, great, Billy! That's the best showing you've made all year!"

**NEVER A LOSER**

Nobody ever gave more of himself, fought more fiercely, and had more confidence in himself than the lion of the pros, Bobby Layne. His old teammate, Doak Walker, expressed it perfectly:

"Bobby never lost a game in his life. Time just ran out on him a few times."

**KNOW DOUBTS**

There's a certain big-time football coach who's a real good man on the practice field but becomes tortured with self-doubt during the actual game. "Once he's made up his mind," dryly remarked a compatriot, "he's full of indecision."

**MONKEYSHINES**

Weeb Ewbank's first official duty with the New York Jets was to set up a tryout camp for all aspiring football players. As you'd expect, the lame, the halt, the blind, and the oddballs turned out by the gross.

Assistant coach George Sauer, the official assorter, shook his head. "I wouldn't be a bit surprised," he said, "if a chimpanzee or two walked in."

**DEATH OF A SALESMAN**

One fellow looked particularly impressive. Coach Sauer

talked to him for 20 minutes, jotting down notes on his age, weight, height, college, and alertness. The coach then shoved the injury waiver sheet across the desk for the fellow's signature.

"I'm sorry, sir," said the visitor, "but I didn't get a chance to explain. I came here to try to sell you some insurance."

**MARITAL LAW**

The sportswriter, noticing the preponderance of married men in the lineup, asked the pro coach if this was just a coincidence.

"No," replied the coach, "I prefer married men. They don't get so upset when I holler at them. They're used to it."

**DEPT. OF HARD KNOX**

Unquestionably, the most bizarre football parent of the century was Harvey Knox, papa of the great quarterback Ronnie Knox. Harvey steered his boy through a half-dozen high schools and colleges, always to the accompaniment of a 40-piece band, shrill cries of murder, and screaming headlines.

Red Sanders, who had his share of hard Knox, put it this way: "I'm going to worry about Harvey after he dies. I'm not altogether sure he's going to like Heaven."

**A RUN
FOR HIS MONEY**

The heroes of the famous 1925 Rose Bowl game between Stanford and Notre Dame had a get-together before the 1963 Stanford-ND game. At one point, the *Indians'* Ernie Nevers turned to the *Fighting Irish's* Elmer Layden and observed:

"I made two of the longest touchdown runs of my career against you."

"Come on, Ernie," Layden snorted, "we beat you 27–10. I don't remember you having any long runs."

"Oh, yes I did," smiled Nevers. "Remember those 80- and 70-yard runs you made after intercepting passes of mine? Who do you think was chasing you?"

**THE BELL RINGO**

Those *Varsity-Alumni* games that wind up so many spring practices these days are interesting, practical, and financially successful affairs. But the poor alumni often take quite a beating, going into the game with just a few days practice. At the last Syracuse *Varsity-Alumni* contest, Coach Ben Schwartzwalder noticed that the alumni's side of the field wasn't fully equipped.

"Jim," he said to the *Alumni* captain (Jim Ringo of the Green Bay *Packers*), "would you like some benches over on your side of the field?"

"Benches, hell," groaned Ringo, "we want cots!"

**SERMON ON THE MOUNT**

The King of Big-Time Football Coaches passed away and in due time arrived at the Pearly Gates. He took his place in line as Saint Peter interviewed the candidates.

The first fellow stepped up and said, "I'm the King of Honesty."

"Can you prove it?" asked Saint Peter. The fellow performed a mighty act of honesty, and Saint Peter let him in.

The next fellow was the King of Truth, who told a mighty truth and was immediately admitted.

The third fellow turned out to be the King of Ethics,

and the fourth was the King of Integrity. Both proved their identity and were admitted to Heaven.

Then it was the turn of the King of Big-Time Football Coaches. He stepped forth and announced, "I'm the King of Big-Time Football Coaches."

"Can you prove it?" asked Saint Peter.

The KBTFC scratched his head. "Gee," he said, "I don't think so."

"Then I don't think I can let you in," Saint Peter said.

"But you let all the other guys in," protested the KBTFC.

"You mean the King of Honesty, the King of Truth, the King of Ethics, and the King of Integrity?"

The Coach shrugged his shoulders, "I never heard of those guys," he said.

Saint Peter threw open the Pearly Gates. "Come on in," he said, "You *must* be the King of Big-Time Football Coaches."

**DEAD CENTER**

In his coaching years at Dartmouth and Boston College, Major Frank Cavanaugh doted on humorous needling, especially of the players he liked the most. Those included three fine centers—Bill Cunningham, Jack Heaphy, and Bill Doyle.

"Heaphy," said Cav one day, "what are you going to do after graduation?"

"I intend to be a teacher and football coach, Major," Jack replied.

"A coach?" boomed Cav incredulously. "Heaphy, how in the name of God are you, a center, ever going to teach football after looking at the game upside down all these years?"

**HARE-RAISING HALFBACK**

Red Sanders had few equals as a football coach, and positively none as a wisecracker.

One afternoon, disgusted at Primo Villanueva's lack of aggressiveness in hitting the line, he impaled Primo with a hard look. "Primo," he drawled, "you sneak up to that line like an Easter bunny."

**SHOT AT DAWN**

During a trip to Illinois, a UCLA tackle, who was a camera bug, kept snapping photos on every occasion. The *Bruins* were beaten by the *Illini*, and on Monday the squad and the coaches sat down for a look at the game film. It showed Johnny Karras, the ace Illinois back, tearing off a huge hunk of yardage while the UCLA tackle stood around bemused.

From out of the dark came Red Sanders' soft drawl, "What's the matter, Bub, forgot your camera?"

**EPIC SILENCE**

Sanders once described the Stanford stands after a UCLA touchdown:

"They were so quiet it was as if a world convention of undertakers had just been informed that somebody had really discovered the secret of eternal life."

**A NOSE FOR TROUBLE**

Bulldog Turner, the great old *Bears'* center, claims that Ed Neal was the only player he could never handle. The forbidding 303-pound *Packer* middle guard broke the Bulldog's nose on four different occasions.

He changed Turner's physiognomy to such an extent that the Big Bear never had much trouble with off-field hecklers.

For example, he once got into a violent argument with a nuisance who apparently was looking for a fight.

"If you think you can whip me," said Turner, advancing, "you can try it."

The opponent took one look at Bulldog's face and retreated. "Maybe I can't whip you," he said, "but apparently somebody else already has."

**THE NORM FOR DISCRETION**

Norm Van Brocklin was pro football's original redneck. Anytime anyone would give him an elbow or a knee, he'd tongue-lash the culprit and, often as not, make an appointment to see the guy after the game.

But there's no record of his ever keeping one of these dates. As Norm explains it, "I may have a hot head, but it's not empty."

**CRIMSON TIDE**

Wally Butts, retired Georgia coach, was telling a football booster how tough Alabama always is. "On our opening kickoff in 1960, they knocked our star fullback for a loop. In fact they not only laid him out cold, they folded his arms!"

**STEVE OWEN'S UP**

Steve Owen was probably the first pro football coach to experiment with the five-man line. The Bears were coming into town and the Giants had to find a way to stop the fabulous Bronko Nagurski. So Coach Owen moved one of his linemen, Hank Reese, back to linebacker.

The game started, and on the first play Nagurski came ramming through. But Reese was right there. He met the Bronk head-on about a yard back.

"Only two things happened that we hadn't counted on," recalls Stout Steve.

"One was that Nagurski made eight yards. The other was that Reese had to be carted off the field. So we got back into our six-man line in a hurry and took our licking."

**(B) LEADERSHIP**

"And remember, men," exhorted the football coach to his high school team, "football develops individuality, leadership, and initiative. Now get out there and do exactly as I tell you."

**FIT TO BE TIED**

It was raining and snowing like crazy when the Cornell and Pennsylvania captains met in the middle of the field for the toss. The Cornell leader called the turn, then bitterly stared out over Franklin Field, covered with a heavy layer of cold, gray slush.

"Do we have to play football in this ocean?" he demanded of the ref.

"Yes," was the implacable reply. "What's your choice?"

"Well," said the player, "we'll kick with the tide."

**SLIGHTLY DANGEROUS**

Bob Devaney, the new football mastermind at Nebraska, has a modest ambition:

"I don't want to win enough games to be put on NCAA probation—just enough to warrant an investigation."

**DOUBLE JEOPARDY**

The ladies auxiliary of the *Rams'* fan club used to reduce Coach Sid Gillman to anguish. One afternoon one of the harpies rose to her feet and asked:

"Mr. Gillman, why do you treat Mr. Van Brocklin like a Charlie McCarthy? Aren't you jeopardizing his job by calling the plays?"

"Lady," Sid snorted, "when he calls the plays he's jeopardizing mine."

**OFF THE HOUK**

Yankee G.M. Ralph Houk, a Kansan football fan, was crestfallen when Colorado, trailing Kansas 19–0 with 10 minutes to go, rallied to win 20–19.

"You should never blow a lead like that," said Houk, the fan.

"Maybe you're going to start yelling for the coach's scalp," he was told.

"Well," replied Houk, "Kansas never would have been ahead like that if not for the coach."

**COUTH AND KEMP(T)**

One of those crackpot TV fans, irritated by Jack Kemp's predilection for running all over the field before heaving a long sideline pass, wrote to the Buffalo quarterback asking him to please keep his passes in range of the TV cameras.

Jackie, ever the gentleman, responded as follows:

"Dear Sir, you have my full sympathy. I'll do my best to develop a 21-inch pass."

**OPTION PLAY**

Sammy Baugh pulled a neat switch on his New York *Titans*. After an extremely rough flight to an exhibition game in Greenville, North Carolina, he informed his squad: "If you beat Houston, you go back home by bus. If you lose, you fly."

**VICTUAL STATISTICS**

When the San Diego *Chargers* came into New York to play the *Titans* in 1962, the local sportswriters traveled to Bear Mountain Inn to confirm Ernie Ladd's caloric capacity.

There they saw the gargantuan tackle (6–9, 305 pounds) consume two shrimp cocktails, three dishes of cole slaw, three spinach servings, three baked potatoes, eight buttered rolls, four 16-ounce steaks, three desserts, and a half-gallon of milk.

Ernie's teammate, Bo Roberson, admonished the writers, who were watching all this with open-mouthed wonder:

"See what you guys have done!"

"What did we do?" asked one of them.

"You got Ernie all upset by watching him eat," replied Bo, "and he's lost his appetite."

**BLANDA'S DREAM HOUSE**

It's been a long while since that day George Blanda sent 90,000 fans home chuckling—at his expense. The *Bears* were trailing the *Rams* 42–38 with about two minutes remaining. On third down, Blanda called a pass play on the snap at two.

But let George take it from here:

"We break out of the huddle and I'm calling the signals: 'Hup one! Hup two!' Everybody explodes except the center and I'm pushing up at him—'Hup three! Hup four!' He turns around and—sure enough, I'm over the guard!"

**COMPARISON SHOPPING**

"Before the season," asserts Ara Parseghian, "I'm often asked how we look. I'm always at a loss as to how to answer. I feel like the man who was asked, 'How's your wife?' and he replied, 'Compared to what?' "

**STAR-SPANGLED BANTER**

Returning to New York after his *Giants* had been annihilated by the *Packers*, 35–0, Coach Allie Sherman was asked to pinpoint the turning point of the championship game.

"It happened," replied Allie with a straight face, "during the playing of the national anthem."

**STOPPED IN HIS TRACKS**

The Big Ten takes its football very seriously indeed.

Some years ago a coach had the misfortune of losing six games in a row. In the lockerroom after the last defeat, the president of the Alumni Association, a compassionate and kindly gentleman, walked over and patted the coach affectionately on the shoulder.

"Coach," he said, "the *Super Chief* pulls out of town in 20 minutes. Be under it."

**CEREBRAL HEMORRHAGE**

College coaches are very academic-grade and IQ conscious in their recruiting these days. The classic story is told by Eddie Crowder, Colorado's football coach.

After finishing a selling job on a brilliant high school

tackle, he was pleased to see the boy smiling and nodding his head.

"Coach," said the boy, "I'd love to come to Colorado. My marks are not so hot, but I'm sure I could pass your college courses."

"What's your IQ?" asked Crowder.

"20–20, Coach," replied the boy.

**POUR LE SPORT**

"The trouble with being a good sport," moans every coach we know, "is that you have to lose to prove you are one."

**LIGHTWEIGHT CHAMPION**

Harvard was demolishing Yale in the 1927 game. With a two-touchdown lead, the *Crimson* coach put in a little fellow named Hammersely. The ball was then on Harvard's 45. The center snapped to Hammersely and the pony back took off around end. His interference swept everything before him. He raced 55 yards without having to change pace, cut, or use a stiff arm.

Benny Friedman, watching the game from the press box, turned to the famed humorist Ring Lardner. "Wasn't that some run!" he enthused. "Did you see him carry that ball! Fifty-five yards!"

Lardner shrugged his shoulders. "Hell," he said, "anybody could do it. It's not that heavy."

**PRO-DIGIOUS EATERS**

The New York *Giants* launched their Professional Quarterbacks Luncheon Club at a renowned Italian restaurant, and the talk turned to the best means of picking the All-Pro team. All sorts of complicated ideas were punted around, until Frank Gifford came up with the simplest solution:

"Any fellow who can eat one of these seven-course Italian lunches and still stand up and take a bow is an All-Pro all the way."

**WARSAW CONCERTO**

Defensive backfield men have a private language when defending against passes. The *Giants*, for example, use cities. "Denver" means one thing, "Omaha" another.

One day, 260-pound tackle Dick Modzelewski volunteered to man a defensive backfield spot in a scrimmage. On the first play he heard Jimmy Patton shout, "Denver!" On the next play Lindon Crow hollered, "Omaha!" On the third play, two receivers came bearing down on Modzelewski.

The rattled Polish lad ransacked his mind for the right call. Finally, in desperation, he sang out, "Warsaw!"

**WRITING CRAMPS**

After watching Lee Grosscup being smeared all over the landscape in his years with the *Giants* and *Jets*, New York football fans didn't exactly send up a rocket over the young quarterback's new book, *Fourth and One*. "A more fitting title," reflected a local sportswriter, "would have been *Second and Seventeen*."

**JUST FOR A CHANGE**

The experts snipe, the fans grouse, but Woody Hayes continues to clippety-clop between the tackles with his famous three-yards-and-a-cloud-of-dust offense. This is the way the Ohio State coach rationalizes:

"This little fellow kept taking a dollar bill to the candy store, getting change for it, taking the change to the bank, and getting a dollar bill for it. Finally the lady in the candy store asked him, 'Listen, what's the big idea?'

"The little fellow smiled. 'One of these days somebody's gonna make a mistake, and it ain't gonna be me.' "

**JUMPING OFF BRIDGERS**

John Bridgers, Baylor football coach, scored a touchdown at an alumni dinner with this nifty pass:

"I realize that Baylor hasn't won a Southwest Conference football championship in 35 years. I assure you that if I don't win it in the next 35 years, I'll bow out gracefully."

**GENERAL PRINCIPLE**

While coaching at Florida, Bob Woodruff was standing on the sidelines one afternoon, puffing on a cigar and chatting with Phil Dickens, the Indiana coach. During a lull in the conversation, they looked up and saw their old coach, the formidable General Bob Neyland, approaching them. Instinctively, Woodruff threw away his cigar.

"What did you do that for?" asked Dickens. "He isn't your boss anymore."

"I know it," answered Woodruff. "But I'm not sure he does."

**NO SNAP OF A JOB**

At the *Raiders'* pre-season camp, Coach Al Davis

noticed one of his rookie tackles practicing the center snap by the hour. Impressed by the boy's attitude, though dismayed by his ineptitude, Davis approached the rookie and asked:

"Say, Bill, why are you, a tackle, practicing all that centering stuff?"

"Coach," replied the boy, "I'm going to take Jim Otto's job."

Davis, who well appreciated the fact that Jim had been the AFL's all-star center for four straight years, shook his head.

"Son," he said dryly, "you talk like a man with a great future behind you."

**MARSHALL MUSIC**

Shirley Povich of *The Washington Post* neatly disposed of George Preston Marshall, the owner of the Washington *Redskins* in this fashion:

"Marshall has authored a football article for the *Saturday Evening Post* and has been the subject of a *Sports Illustrated* story. He is getting more publicity than any loser since Robert E. Lee."

**DON ON THE QUARTERBACK**

In this last season with the *Giants*, Don Heinrich was having a nightmare afternoon against the Cleveland *Browns*. He just couldn't hit a receiver and was being intercepted all over the lot. Late in the final quarter, he attempted to hit an end on an in-and-out pattern. The end seemed to catch the ball momentarily, then, as he was hit, the ball popped up—and into a defensive halfback's hands.

The official statistician was in a dilemma:

"Would you call that a fumble, or an intercepted pass?" he asked a nearby reporter.

The scribe, a *Giant* fan at heart, cynically sneered, "An interception, of course. Heinrich threw it, didn't he?"

**LETTER TO A NAVE**

With time running out and Duke winning 3–0 in the 1939 Rose Bowl game, USC threw in a fourth-string back named Doyle Nave. The unknown sub promptly started flinging the ball all over the lot, winding up with a last-second toss for the winning touchdown.

Back in the tumultuous dressing room, all that Nave could say was, "Gee, I wonder if I'll get a letter now."

"Son," he was told, "you're going to get the whole alphabet."

**INVISIBLE, INC.**

Everyone who saw Vic Turyn, the Maryland quarterback, fake Georgia into knots in the 1948 Gator Bowl went away convinced that Vic was the greatest prestidigitator since Houdini. At one stage of the game, he faked to two backs before tucking the ball into Lu Gambino's stomach. Lu rambled 25 yards before he was felled.

Turyn feigned annoyance when Gambino returned to the huddle:

"You big ox," he snapped, "you get 25 yards when you should have had a touchdown."

"It wasn't my fault," groaned the big halfback. "I didn't even know I had the ball until I was tackled."

### GENTEEL LYNCHING

A football coach who once coached in the rough West but was now coaching in the staid East was discussing his career to a sportswriter:

"When I lose, they still hang me in effigy, but here in the East my head is constructed by an Art major."

### BANANA EARL

Earl Morrall, the Detroit *Lions'* quarterback, was the guest on a radio program after winning a game with a 79-yard toss to Dave Middleton.

Asked to describe this sensational play, the former Michigan State All-American stunned one and all with this highly professional analysis:

"It's our 8-look-in, which is like a bend-in deep with green left slow. It's not much more than a back dividing to the left, or the same as a swing-in the left. This time we did it off our opposite, making it from a 2 right. Any questions?"

### DOWN TO EARTH

At the awards banquet following the 1963 Gator Bowl in which Florida beat Penn State, 17–7, the *Nittany Lions'* president, Eric A. Walker, pointed out the difference between winning and losing.

"Last year, when we won, I sat next to Miss America. Today we're the losers, and I'm sitting next to my wife."

### DEAD TO RIGHTS

Upon learning that a team from a tiny college in Washington, Pennsylvania, had been selected to play mighty

California in the 1922 Rose Bowl game, a Pacific Coast sports editor shook his head and moaned:

"The only thing I know about Washington and Jefferson is that both are dead."

### A TIME TO CROWLEY

Sleepy Jim Crowley was easily the star of the 1925 Rose Bowl game, tallying three touchdowns, two of them on long run-backs of intercepted passes (78 yards and 70 yards). After his second long run broke up the game, Knute Rockne took him out amidst a tremendous ovation.

"I know why you're taking me out, Coach," Crowley said when he reached the bench. "You saw it."

"Saw what?" demanded the puzzled Notre Dame perfectionist.

"Why, on that last run I carried the ball under the wrong arm."

### THE STUFF DREAMS ARE MADE OF

Even his teammates on the *Redskins* held Sammy Baugh in awe. Once a huge, muscular rookie trying out for the team was introduced to Sammy.

"Gee," he practically blushed, "I always dreamed of playing with the great Sammy Baugh, and now it's gonna come true."

"What position do you play?" Baugh asked.

"Tackle," answered the youth.

"Well, you knock the dickens out of some of those linemen and I'll dream of *you*," Sammy responded.

**GETS YOU IN THE END**

Several years ago, Ray W. Ballock was leading his Orland, California, high school team through a conditioning drill.

"Boys, I want you to remember this," he emphasized, "it's the *last* five push-ups you do that really count."

One of the guards, Ken Yost, looked up from his prone position. "Coach," he said, "if you'll skip the first thirty we'll work real hard on the last five."

**DON'TS AND DO'S**

Roger Hudnill, coach at Waterloo High, New Marshfield, Ohio, compiled this model list of training habits for the non-athlete:

DON'TS

1. Eat pizza.
2. Eat spaghetti and meatballs.
3. Smoke.
4. Drink a carton of pop every day.
5. Always ask for second helpings.

DO'S

1. Do all the don'ts.

**LEAGUES APART**

The AFL is constantly importuning the NFL for a football World Series, which the NFL completely rejects. Sid Gillman, Charger coach who's an old buddy of Pete Rozelle, NFL Commissioner, recently tried to push the game with the following telegram to Rozelle:

POPE JOHN XXIII WAS A GREAT MAN. HE RECOGNIZED THE OTHER LEAGUE [*meaning the other faiths*].

Rozelle promptly wired back:

TRUE, BUT IT TOOK 2,000 YEARS.

**WHITE MAN'S BURDICK**

Enthused by the results of the intensive isometric program introduced at the San Diego *Chargers'* pre-season camp in Boulevard, California—cradle of the American rattlesnake—publicity director Bob Burdick proudly announced that, after a lifetime of dedication to ennui, "I've begun working on the weights and isometrics myself and the results have been fantastic. I've already broken three typewriters."

**CHE-RUBICK SPARTAN**

Squat, stubby Ron Rubick, a 5–7, 185-pound Michigan State halfback, definitely isn't the distance-running type. Chided by Coach Duffy Daugherty for not doing well in the mile-run conditioning drill, Rubick replied:

"Coach, you gotta remember I have to take twice as many steps as anyone else."

**RETURN OF THE NATIVE**

Among the notables at the opening of pro football's Hall of Fame were Jimmy Conzelman and Joe Guyon, who played with the Carlisle *Indians* before becoming outstanding pros. When the famous guests were asked to line up, Conzelman stepped briskly to the head of the line. He immediately was tapped on the shoulder.

"Just a minute," said Guyon. "Natives first."

**ON SCHEDULE**

The clinic director noticed one of the veteran coaches walking around the tables in the lunch room. "What's the idea of moving around so much?" he asked.

"I'm looking for the coaches who are drinking milk," was the explanation. "They're the guys who must have the ulcers, and that means they mustn't have too much coming back. Those are the boys I want to schedule."

**FAMILY DINNER**

Ralph Guglielmi, who must have about 2,000 plays and variations stockpiled in his brain, yearns to play quarterback for the *Chinese Bandits*.

"Think how simple it would be," he says, "if you have a choice of only one from Column A and two from Column B."

**TAYLOR:**
**CLEANING AND DYING**

Back in his rookie year with the Chicago *Bears*, Lionel Taylor almost wore the skin off both hands catching passes in practice. All he wanted was a chance to show his stuff. Sure enough, late in the last quarter of the *Bears*' first exhibition game, the call finally came.

Lionel adjusted his helmet, loosened up, and stepped up to Coach George Halas for instructions.

"We've run out of time-outs, Taylor," Halas snapped. "Go in and get hurt."

**BLOCK-BOARD**

Abner Haynes, the explosive halfback of the K. C. *Chiefs*, was asked if his feats of derring-do made him vulnerable to a swelled head.

"No," replied Abner, "not before I talk it over with the guards."

**GREASY KID STUFF**

Irrepressible Bobby Layne says his ambition is to do a TV commercial with the *Giants'* Y. A. Tittle.

"First you see me trying to pass and I get knocked down by Sam Huff. Then you see Tittle clobbered by Ernie Stautner. The scene then shifts to the dressing room where Tittle says to me, 'Are you still using that greasy kid stuff?'

"I take a moment combing my full head of hair, look at Tittle's bald head, and say, 'Of course I am.'

"Tittle shakes his head and answers, 'I wish I'd listened to you 20 years ago.' "

**SPREE DE CORPSE**

The *Giants* and *Browns* staged a wild scoring spree in the last game of the 1962 season. The *New York Daily Mirror* man covering the game described it this way:

> **The way the clubs were throwing and scoring in the early going, someone must've sneaked in a 24-second clock and a few NBA refs, too. There was constant charging and blocking foul confusion on pass play. Man, what Red Auerbach could've done with such material.**

**Virginia State's snappy band turned in the sock halftime show of the season. It's such a fast-stepping outfit, it played the 15-minute intermission in 7½.**

**DARNED WITH THE WIND**

Bob Zuppke and Knute Rockne carried on a hilarious feud in the great football years of the 1920's. At one sports dinner, Rockne said with mock modesty:

"My assistants do all the coaching. All I do is blow up the footballs."

Whereupon Zuppke arose and said:

"I'd like to do that too. But I don't have so much wind."

**RIVERBOAT GAMBLER**

Shortly after two horrible plane crashes in New York, Pappy Lewis, former West Virginia football coach, appeared at the ticket window in the Morgantown airport. "Miss," he said to the young lady, "I'll take two chances to New York."

**IN A MINER KEY**

When an NCAA investigation disclosed that the team's star tackle had been recruited from a mining town in an under-cover deal involving $3,000 cash and $100 a week during the school year, the local sports columnist dipped his quill in poison and wrote:

"Shouldn't our beloved college be hit with the book for contributing to the delinquency of a miner?"

**FIRING UP THE BEARS**

The Chicago *Bears* had been something of a bust (until 1963), and the natives were getting restless. When a fire swept the *Bears'* office, destroying many valuable records and plays, one of the local critics heaved a sigh of satisfaction.

"Well," he said, "that's about the only way you could have got 'em to come up with a new offense."

**SECOND HUFF RALLY**

Sam Huff, the *Redskin* linebacker who's supposed to "own" Jimmy Brown, tells a nice story about the crunching *Browns'* fullback. It seems Jimmy was busting up the middle too frequently in one of these *Giants–Browns* donnybrooks. So Sam decided to try some psychology—believing it might persuade Jimmy to try the ends for a change.

The next few times Jimmy came barging up the middle, Sam hit him hard, laid on him, and grunted:

"Brown, you stink."

Each time Jimmy gave him a funny look, but didn't say a word. Came a third-down situation with long yardage to go, and Sam edged back to cover for a pass. But, to his surprise, Brown was sprung up the middle on a trap. He went 65 yards for a touchdown, with Sam in hot pursuit.

As Jimmy crossed the goal line, he looked over his shoulder and casually remarked, "Tell me, Sam, how do I smell from here?"

**IDIOT'S DELIGHT**

The second-string quarterback, attempting to make a

deposit in the local bank, was sharply reprimanded for filling out his deposit slip improperly. When he returned later, after rectifying his error, the teller apologized to him.

"Oh, that's all right," said the boy. "I'm the second-string quarterback at school, so I'm used to being spoken to as if I were an idiot."

**FRIGHT TRAIN**

Tommy Harmon and Johnny Lujack made a most felicitous combination for the telecast of the 1962 Cotton Bowl Game between Texas and Mississippi. During one time-out, Johnny was elaborating on the difference between pure running speed and quickness. Finally, he turned to Harmon, perhaps the greatest running back in Michigan history.

"Say, Tommy," he said, "were you fast or quick?"

"Just scared, Johnny," was the quick rejoinder.

**FLUID DRIVE**

Perhaps the best "line" in the 1961 Playoff Bowl game was neither the *Eagles*' nor the *Lions*'. It was Pete Retzlaff's. After the *Eagles* had absorbed that 38–10 licking, the veteran *Eagle* end sighed:

"We figured in only one drive all day. And that was on the bus to the Orange Bowl."

**BURNED AT THE STEAK**

Seems the football *Giants* were in their third day of pre-season conditioning one year at the Bear Mountain (New York) Inn, when the Inn manager, Jack Martin, walked into the dining room and sat down with Coach Steve Owen.

He asked Stout Steve to point out some of the rookies. "That big fellow over there, who's he?"

Steve scratched his head. "I don't know. How the devil do you expect me to remember the names of all these new kids?"

Martin grinned back. "You'd better know this. He's not a football player, but he has been eating steaks on you for three days."

**A PERFECT LIE**

The worried mother took her child to a psychiatrist to find out what she could do about his lying.

"Do nothing," advised the head shrinker. "Just let him grow up and he'll get a good job as a football recruiter."

**"A" FOR EFFORT**

Woody Hayes' son, Steve, came home from school with a beaming face. "Look, Dad," he exclaimed, holding out his report card. The Ohio State coach looked—and saw three A's and two B's.

"It's fine, Steve," he said, but, ever the perfectionist, he added, "But don't you think it could stand some improvement?"

The boy's head fell, and Woody realized he had made a mistake. "I'm sorry, Steve," he said, trying to make amends. "But I was visiting with Bud Wilkinson last week, and he told me that his son, Jay, had made straight A's."

A twinkle appeared in Steve Hayes' eyes. "Yes, Dad," he said, "but Jay Wilkinson's father won 45 straight games."

**WOODY'S FINE TOUCH**

"I always try to make a prospect welcome," says Woody

Hayes. "I always go up to him, give him a big hello, shake his hand, and clap him on the shoulder—*then slide my hand down his arm.*"

**SULLIVAN'S JOHN L.**

"We were playing the conference champs, Sullivan High, and not doing so well," writes Coach Dan Sonnenberg of Cerro Gordo, Illinois, High School.

"At the half, they had us down 38–0. And it could have been worse. To keep the score down, Sullivan was kicking on first down and trying field goals from the 45-yard line.

"This was the time to give everyone on the bench some 'experience.' So, early in the second half, we put in one of our perennial bench-warmers. The kid he replaced came running to the bench.

" 'Coach,' he said, 'you better get Johnny out of there. He's real mad. He's going to hurt somebody in there."

**A MATTER OF SENIORITY**

Arlington State was taking a drubbing in an NAIA game, and the quarterback kept coming to the sidelines to talk to the coach. Having enough trouble the way it was, Coach Chena Gilstrap always managed to busy himself somewhere whenever he saw the boy approaching.

Finally the quarterback shouted so loudly that Gilstrap couldn't ignore him. "It's third and eight. What do you want me to do?"

"You're on a four-year scholarship, and I have a one-year contract," snarled Gilstrap. "You call it!"

**NOT SO DUMMY**

The rough old team trainer looked dolorous as the team took the field for its opening game against SMU.

"What's bothering you, Mike?" queried a sportswriting friend.

"We're not ready," grunted the tape-strapper. "We haven't had enough live scrimmaging. Nothing but all that dummy drill."

Then he brightened. "But I'll say this. If we ever run up against a team of dummies, we'll sure stomp hell out of 'em!"

**TOSS OF THE KERN**

Bill Kern, the old Carnegie Tech coach, once told Harry Stuhldreher that he played tackle for the Green Bay *Packers* at 180 pounds, while Cal Hubbard, the other tackle, tipped the beam at 280.

"That," replied Harry with a straight face, "must have been the start of the unbalanced line."

**ANCIENT SPORTS**

The football coach of a little athletic foundry insisted on paying lip service to academic standards. He wouldn't pass out a uniform until the boy passed a one-question test, to wit:

"Name two ancient sports."

The only athlete ever to win his letter without playing a down was the one who pondered the question for several moments and then answered, "Anthony and Cleopatra."

**BUILDING PROJECT**

Having just hired a new football coach, the Chairman of the Athletic Board popped the big question:

"Coach, how long will it take you to produce a winner?"

"Oh, about three years," replied the new head man.

"Three years!" echoed the Chairman in dismay. "Why, the good Lord took only six days to create the whole world."

"That's true," snapped the coach, "but have you taken a good look at it lately?"

**COACH IN A FUHRER**

"Now, gentlemen," said the new head coach, addressing his staff for the first time, "I have a suggestion about a change in our system for the coming year, and I'd like to hear all your opinions about it. Those opposed to my little idea can signify by saying, ' I resign.' "

**THE STRAIGHT AND NARROW**

At the last convention of the football coaches association, a coach of a small, non-scholarship school buttonholed one of the famous big-time mentors.

"There are many ways to develop a winner," he declared, "but there's only one honest way."

"And what's that?" demanded the big-time operator.

"Aha!" smiled the first, "I thought you wouldn't know!"

**WATER, WATER EVERYWHERE**

The 1960 George Washington University team worked out on a field right next to a canal. "We could never throw to the right for fear of getting someone drowned," reported Coach Bob Faris. "We were the only team in the nation with a trainer and a lifeguard."

**TURNING ON THE FANS**

With a World Series game scheduled for Yankee Stadium on Sunday, the lovable Harry Wismer thought he could hitch-hike onto all the excitement in town by scheduling a *Titan–Patriot* football game for Saturday night. Like all of the Lovable One's promotions, this one laid a big fat egg. About 50 people were in the Polo Grounds as the *Titans* took the field.

Captain Larry Grantham winced as he surveyed the "crowd." He turned to his teammates:

"Fellers," he said, "they're gonna do something new tonight. Instead of introducing the players to the fans, they're gonna introduce the fans to the players."

**HARRY MISSES THE POINTS**

After three smashing defeats, Harry Wismer called in six of his better players.

"Gentlemen," he announced, "if we don't win our next two games in Texas, our season will be lost. We're giving up too many points. San Diego got 40, Denver got 32, and Boston got 43. That's an average of about 50 points a game."

**CAUGHT BEAR**

A new twist on an oldie, currently popular in the Southeastern Conference:

It seems Bear Bryant was in Moscow to lecture on football. Near the end of his talk, Khrushchev came in and sat down in the last row. After the lecture, Mr. K. invited the tall, powerful Bear to inspect one of the new Russian factories. Bryant accepted, and soon they were walking down a row of glittering machines.

The workers gathered in a nearby corner. One nudged the other and asked:

"Comrade, who is that fat little fellow with Bear Bryant?"

**HEN PARTY**

Did you hear about the football coach who had to quit because he developed such a terrible persecution complex? Every time the players went into a huddle, he thought they were talking about him.

**WRONG NUMBER**

Trying to pull the Baylor game out of the fire, Texas Tech coach DeWitt Weaver kept up a feverish telephone conversation with his spotters in the press box.

One of the coeds in the stand looked at him with disgust. "No wonder we're losing," she snorted. "Our coach spends all his time on the phone."

**WISMER WHILE YOU WORK**

We miss Harry Wismer on the air. As an announcer, Harry was always good for a howl.

We can still hear him, his voice pulsing like an overheated motor:

"He's on the 30, the 35, the 40, the 45, the 50, *the 55!*"

And then there was the time he was describing a field goal attempt:

"He kicks! And it's a beautiful kick! End-over-end! Terrific! *And it's no good!*"

**LIFE OF RILEY**

When the *Redskins* moved from Boston to Washington, 12,000 fans came out to see them play the *Giants*. The local fans had eyes only for the fabulous Cliff Battles and the sharpshooter, Sammy Baugh. But it was Riley Smith, the blocking back, who stole all the thunder. He intercepted a pass and ran for a 60-yard touchdown, converted the extra point, then kicked two field goals. The final score was Riley Smith 13, *Giants* 3.

In the chronicles that review the *Redskins'* history, the team historian pays obeisance to Riley in this fashion:

"In the *Redskins'* first game in Washington, Secretary of Commerce Jesse Jones threw out the first ball, and Riley Smith played with it all night."

**DIRTY POOL**

Whimsical Duffy Daugherty was asked about the new pool table he had just installed in the game room of his home.

"It's mainly for my kids," the Michigan State coach explained. "I want them to have the same start in life that I did."

**ALLIE OOPS**

"Win one for the Old Gipper" has become a legendary byword at Notre Dame. The New York *Giants* invented their own version of it last season. It seems that the owner of a Long Island chain of lox-and-bagel stores offered the *Giant* players free samples of these delicacies as an inducement to beat the hated *Browns*.

"All right," Coach Allie Sherman is reported to have told his *Giants* shortly before the kickoff, "let's win one for the old kipper."

**A FINE TIME**

Back in his coaching days with the Green Bay *Packers*, Curly Lambeau had an automatic fine of $500 for anyone who missed practice. One afternoon four of the monsters failed to show up, and Lambeau promptly fined them $500 apiece. As the players started writing out the checks, Curly read their minds.

"I'm cashing them, too," he said, "before you can stop payment."

A big lineman grabbed Curly by the shoulder and snarled, "If you cash my check I'll kill you."

"It won't do you any good," the coach replied. "I'll just fine you another $500."

**KNOCKED 'EM SPEECHLESS**

The team's star tackle, a fellow with broad shoulders

and a low brow, was prevailed upon to take a course in public speaking. "It's a snap," he was assured. In his first day in class, he was called upon to make a five-minute speech.

He broke into a cold sweat as he struggled to his feet, stood there silently for 30 seconds, then said:

"Ladies and gentlemen, let's all bow our heads for five minutes of silent prayer."

**EXIT CHATTERING**

Duffy Daugherty is such a funny guy that pro scouts insist that every player he produces is a fierce blocker, a savage tackler, and a helluva comedian.

One year he had a hard time whee-ing up Michigan State for a below-par Notre Dame eleven.

"All right, laugh if you want to," he warned his team. "But over there across the field, Terry Brennan is dragging up the ghost of every football hero Notre Dame ever had. You'll be playing the Four Horsemen, and maybe even George Gipp."

Clarence Peaks, the big fullback, tittered.

"Look here, Peaks," Duffy glowered, "I'm not kidding. Tell me, are you gonna let George Gipp tackle you today?"

"Coach," Peaks replied, pointing at a spot in the grandstand, "if George Gipp comes into this stadium—*that exit is mine!*"

**IT'S A GIPP**

Notre Dame did surprisingly well for the first half, helped no end by the MSU center who, at a critical point, sailed the ball over the punter's head.

"Son," Duffy said at halftime, "how could you do something like that?"

"Coach, I know you're going to tell me I'm nuts, but just before I went to snap the ball, it moved."

"Hey," shouted a sub, "it must have been George Gipp reaching up."

"Have a little respect!" Duffy snapped. "If it was George Gipp, you can be assured he was reaching down—not up."

**GETTING UP STEAM**

As a valve in the dormitory steam boiler near the Michigan State practice field suddenly started issuing a loud hiss of escaping steam, Duffy Daugherty stopped practice and listened for a while. Then he turned to a group of bystanders and remarked:

"Do you suppose it could be the alumni warming up for the new season?"

**THE HOUSE OF MORGAN**

Rex Morgan played football at Penn before turning actor.

"I went to Penn before they gave up football," he says. "George Munger was the coach then. You remember him. He was later tried as a war criminal by the alumni. There certainly have been some changes made in Penn football. I'm surprised to hear they now speak English in the huddles. When I was there, they spoke to the ends in Polish, the tackles in Italian, and just grunted and pointed straight ahead for the guards and center."

**MAKRIS OF DEATH**

George Makris, Temple's football coach, attended his

University's annual journalism clinic for Pennsylvania high school students. Just before the clinic signed off, a budding newspaperman signified that he had one more question.

"Coach Makris," he said, "you've just signed a three-year contract. Do you expect to be here four years from now?"

### REAL ESTATE VALUES

Who was it that said, "The greatest piece of real estate in football is the six inches between the quarterback's ears"?

### IN A BIT OF A DAIS

Joe Bellino played out his three years at Navy with hardly an injury. But, attending a big sports banquet after his last game, he came a cropper. Seating himself at the dais, Bellino caught a finger under the loose seat of his chair, drawing blood from under the nail.

"Well," philosophized Joe, "that's show business."

### THE RING OF TRUTH

After the *Chargers* destroyed the *Patriots* for the 1963 AFL championship, Coach Sid Gillmann doled out rings to every man on the squad. Inscribed on the inside was "San Diego *Chargers,* Champions of the World, 1963."

A friendly newspaperman kidded the coach:

"Sid," he said, "is that inscription really accurate? After all, don't the *Bears* have just as much right to it?"

Sid remained unruffled:

"Look," he said, "if the *Bears* want to object, tell 'em we'll play 'em for it."

**THE WAY HARRY WOULDA DONE IT!**

Before leaving this vale of tears and rabbit punches, the late lamented Harry Balough, boxing announcer extraordinary, paralyzed many a fistic audience with his Ciceronian mutilation of the English language.

Undisputed world's heavyweight champion of malapropism, redundancy, and sesquipedalianism (when accused of the latter, Harry stoutly averred, asserted, and vouchsafed that he was positively tolerant of all kinds of people, regardless of race, color or creed), the Great Verce contributed a unique absurdity to the boxing scene, and his passing left a hole—or as Harry would say, an abbess—that nobody has been able to fill.

Tuning in on the TV football game-of-the-week one Saturday afternoon, we suddenly thought of Harry as we watched the dull, stilted, pre-game charade between the captains and the head official. "Oh what Harry could have done with *this* opportunity!" we thought. The Great Man would have invested the toss-up of the coin with a grandeur and excitement that probably would have gone something like this . . .

**"Captain Bolling, meet your courageous and fearless adversary, weighing two-oh-five-and-a-quarter pounds and wearing the purple and white trunks of that gridiron capital of the Mojave Desert, Braille University—Captain O'Connor.**

**"Captain O'Connor, this scrappy, lion-hearted warrior in the silver and blue trunks, weighing one-ninety-eight-and-a-h-a-a-a-alf, formerly a native of the great little football town of Chickamauga, now battling out of Slavverd College, Captain Bolling.**

"Gentlemen, I presume you're aware of, conversant with, and apprehensive of the fact that this contest is being waged under the auspices, aegis, and sponsorship of the National Collegiate Ath-a-letic Association, and that the officials have been chosen and selected by your grand little conference that embraces the seven great states abutting and bordering our great good neighbor to the North, Saskatchewan, and that historic and legendary pride of the golden wheat country to the south, Death Valley.

"Gentlemen, are you ready for the propelment of the kern—oops, coin? Captain Bolling, as the visiting visitor it's your call. You call posterior. Here's the propelment. Captain Bolling, I regret, rue, and lament this moment. The kern—er, coin has come up anterior.

"Captain O'Connor, what is your desire and wish? You choose to receive the oblate spheroid.

"Captain Bolling, what corner will you defend with that great little fighting heart that has made you the toast of six betting syndicates and two girls' dormitories? The north corner? A wise, judicious, even perspicacious decision—congratulations and feliciations, Captain Bolling!

"Gentlemen, are there any questions about the rules? What's that, Captain O'Connor? No! I don't think that Captain Bolling's fists are encased with more than the eight pounds of plaster of paris permitted under the official code and rules of the NCAA. You think he's wearing brass knuckles under his bandages?

"Fie, shame, Captain O'Connor! Captain Bolling is an honest and honorable American from a great little school universally renowned and acclaimed for its sportsmanship, scholarship, and dignified panty raids. He'd never be a party to such a fraudulent and deceitful piece of deceitfulness.

"What's that, Captain Bolling? You'd like to know why Captain O'Connor's headgear is festooned with bayonets? Now come, Captain Bolling, you know that this is fair Slavverd's Homecoming Day for Veterans of Foreign Wars—the bayonets are just part of the showmanship for this glorious event and occasion. That's show biz, Captain Bolling.

"Any more questions? None? That's the spirit, gentlemen.

"Now, before you shake heads and come out clipping, I want you to understand that this contest is being relayed over that marvelous and wonderful miracle of modern science, television. That means that 22 million freedom-loving, non-communistic Americans from the rock-bound beaches of California to the sunny, balmy, mist-shrouded cliffs of Nova Scotia will be tuned in on your contestation of strength, agility, and celibation. Leave us give them a real good, clean, American kind of contest.

"Now shake heads like real, genuine sportsmen and the best of luck to both of you—*watch that butting, Captain Bolling!*

"Just a moment, just a moment, gentlemen. I apperceive a representative of the XYZ network running out to have a word with us.

"Mr. Susskind, it's a pleasure, a joy, and a treat to meet you on such a memorable occasion. I'd like to introduce you to Captain . . . What's that, sir? The network has already used up the three hours it had slotted for this contest? Good grief, good heavens, great Daniel Parker. I'm embarrassed, nonplussed, and rendered almost speechless. I hardly know what to . . . .

"What's that, you say? It's perfectly all right? What . . . what . . . what . . . they loved ME on TV!"

## LAMENT OF A WHISTLE WIDOW

*By Elizabeth Sandlin*
*Duncan, Oklahoma*

***"My husband is a referee."***

It's surprising how such a simple statement can shake up people. It's guaranteed to produce a long moment of silence, while everyone frantically gropes for something nice to say.

Rarely does anyone succeed. Who can think of anything nice to say about a referee? Unless, of course, you happen to be the wife of one—as I am.

Not that it's any picnic. I spend my "finest hours" washing and ironing linen pants, black-and-white striped shirts, and all the other bizarre accoutrements of his trade.

And what is my reward? Solitary confinement. While the man of the house is out blowing whistles in front of crowds, I'm anchored to the hearth. As a friend of mine says, "Call me Toni. I'm home permanent."

After three fourths of the season is over and you think you can't bear another night of putting the kids to bed and watching TV or trying to get up all-girl bridge foursomes, you decide to brave one more game and go with him. That's when your trouble really begins.

When our children were pre-schoolers, I took them with me to a lot of games. I didn't have to worry about bed-time schedules or homework, and it seemed better than spending the evening at home. So every other game or so, I went along.

That's all you could call it—"went along." "Tagged along" would probably be more appropriate. Because referees generally go in pairs—or, to make it worse, in three's.

It's easier for the school footing the bill to pay only one car's mileage. So the principal usually manages to hire three men from the same general locality for football, and two for basketball. But it always seems to be football games with which I become entangled.

Anyway, you hurry through supper and get the children dressed.

Who can pay a baby sitter for an out-of-town ballgame which may involve some four or five hours? That'll eat up the profits. So, with your husband prodding you every minute to hurry, you jump frantically in the car, only to discover you've forgotten your crossword puzzle book and the candy bars for the children.

Then you pick up the other two officials, who come lumbering to the car in their unwieldy, spiked shoes, hobble into the seat, and turn around to give you a forced, gallant smile. After that word of greeting and a pleasantry to the children, they turn around.

And you've had it for the rest of the evening.

The talk for the next twenty—or thirty, or fifty—miles consists of single wings, T or spread formations, number of yards per penalty, and the disposition, ancestry, and general IQ of all the coaches in the region.

You settle the children's arguments, rearrange your hair, put on your lipstick, and try to take an intelligent interest in the conversation.

Which is another thing. Very few officials' wives know a foul from a hen party. But we try. (Don't we all read the articles that tell us to be interested in our husbands' hobbies?) But it's all rather difficult, like learning a foreign language or learning to skate before you can walk.

Finally you're there, and now your life's mate must apologetically explain to the man at the gate that ". . . this is my wife and children."

The explanation has to be made, or else said wife and children would have to pay admission and to be forced to *pay* for the horrors you're about to experience is unthinkable.

At most high school football games, a few cars, including the officials', are allowed inside the field. So now you're faced with the decision either to sit in the car and work crossword puzzles, provided you remembered the book, or to take the children and go sit in the empty stands.

Of course they are empty. No one in his right mind, except a referee, would dream of arriving an hour before game time.

Usually, since the children insist, we go sit in the stands. We watch the visiting team's bus arrive and the boys emerge. We hear shouts and laughter from the dressing rooms. We watch the harrowing bustle of the teachers operating the concession stands, and the antics of the students supposedly assisting them. We see the band members arrive and hear the screech of tuning instruments.

I always try to sit on the side of the home team. I have several reasons for this.

For one thing, the conversation is usually more interesting. I can hear the latest gossip—learn who's been canning preserves this week, who is worn out from car pools, and what the doctor's wife is wearing tonight.

Also, since the home team has done the hiring (with the approval, of course, of the visiting team) the home fans are a little—but only a little—less prone to criticize.

Which actually means that it generally takes them until the second quarter to start booing the officials, whereas the visitors begin the moment those striped-shirt "enemies" walk out onto the field to toss the coin.

And the last—and most important reason—is that there are usually more hot-coffee urns in the concession stands on the home team's side than there are in the visitor's bleachers.

Finally, after endless waiting and fidgeting, and at least one trip to the rest room with the children and repeated refusals of Cokes, candy, peanuts, popcorn, and snow cones ("No, you know you can't eat until the half"), the bleachers are finally full.

The two teams have been exercising, punting, blocking, and running all over the field for at least forty-five minutes, and the coaches have worn down one set of fingernails apiece. Now the three officials stroll leisurely out onto the field, your spouse among them.

Sometimes the fans are more interested in who's

going to be captain for this game, or what a monster that visiting captain is ("Looks like he's 21 if he's a day!"), or even which team will win the toss. But most of the time you're not so lucky. It's the referees they're interested in. And here's where is starts:

"Who are the referees?"

"I hope it's not that idiot we had last week."

"Oh, one of them is that blind bat from Elmwood."

"There's that red-headed one. Have they got him again?"

Now, *that's* the statement I've been waiting for: my husband is red-headed. I don't know why a crowd will always pick on a red-head, but they do. Probably because he's the one they can tag with a name. At least that's what I keep telling myself.

"Isn't he the prissiest thing?" the woman behind me demands. "Just look at him. You'd think he owned the place."

"Which one?" asks her neighbor.

"That red-headed one. Seems like he's here every game. I don't know why they keep hiring him."

I sit perfectly still and don't breathe. The children, miraculously, haven't heard.

Then suddenly they're off. The game has finally begun, and all you have to do from here on out is to sit still, keep the children from falling on somebody's head, and show a semblance of interest and intelligence.

It helps when you have a son to explain it to you. Since the time when Timmie was four, some five years ago, he has known more about football than I do. I get even with him during basketball season. *That's* my game.

But as to football, I'm lost.

"What happened?" I whisper furtively, as fifteen helmeted lads untangle themselves on the field, the umpire goes over to pick up his red flag, and the crowd is on its collective feet, screaming insults at the officials.

"They were off side. Didn't you see the red flag?" Timmie yells.

"Sh!" I warn him. "Not so loud. Which team was off side?"

"Bellmont, of course, Mother. Don't you remember? I told you they had the red jerseys."

By this time the crowd has turned its attention from the erring referees to us, and quiet amusement is written over several faces.

The whispering begins:

"Who are *they?*"

"I don't know."

"They must be from Pinedale. I never saw them before."

I sit up straighter and feign absorption in the game, being most careful all the while to yell for neither team.

Would that my children were so careful. When the first player runs out onto the field, they begin taking sides, each dickering and swaying until they can discover which team the other one is for.

When Sally finally chooses Pinedale, Timmie decides his team is Bellmont. They've been warned, since they first learned to toddle up a stadium step, not to verbally support any particular team. But in the heat of battle, their enthusiasm runs away with them, and they cheer and boo as loud as any partisan spectator.

I endure it, somehow, through the first quarter, wishing desperately for a cup of coffee. But if I buy one now, that'll mean I'll have to get something for the children. At that rate, I'll be out thirty cents a quarter, even a dollar twenty a game. Again, that's eating up the profits. So I wait.

The second quarter drags along. Both teams get penalized many times. I've learned all about penalties. Well, at least all I'm interested in learning. When a team is penalized, it stops the clock. And each time the clock is stopped, the game is delayed just that much longer. Therefore, I'm against penalties.

All at once I can stand it no longer without coffee. So I buy a cup from a passing boy, along with two boxes of popcorn. This occupies me for five more minutes.

Then, suddenly, it's the half.

The boys lope off the field, the band comes marching on. Sally jumps up excitedly to watch her idols, the twirlers. I'm happily keeping time with the music, when I look over just in time to see Timmie frantically waving to someone just below.

Here are the three officials, Coke bottles in

hand, strolling back from the concession stand. As they near us, the crowd grows silent and watchful, critically surveying their every move.

Timmie rises to his feet.

"Hello, Daddy! Hello, Daddy! Look, here's where we are! Sally, wave to Daddy!"

I make a grab for Sally, but I'm too late. She jumps up on the seat and waves merrily.

"Hello, Daddy!" she calls. "I've been watching you!"

Red turns around, smiles wanly, and waves his hand.

"That's my Daddy!" Sally happily informs everyone around us.

I feel all eyes upon me. There's a dead silence. I carefully empty my coffee cup and set it on the seat beside me.

The lady who was obsessed with "prissy redheads" begins to giggle. A gradual crescendo of whispers and giggles builds up behind me. Someone cautions the others to silence, and stifled sputters follow.

"Come on, children, it's time to go to the car," I announce. "We can see just as well from there, and it'll be lots warmer."

Amid their protests and tears, I gather up coats, scarfs, gloves, programs, and popcorn boxes, and usher them quickly down the steps. As I reach the bottom and turn toward the car, the crowd—unable to contain itself any longer—breaks into one loud mass hysteria.

"Oh well," I rationalize, "if I've forgotten the crossword puzzle book, I can always clean out the car pocket. Come along, children."

## NOT AT ALL-AMERICAN

*By Jim Murray*
*Syndicated Sports Columnist*

It's that time of year again. The AP, the UPI, *Playboy* magazine—every publication but the Dead Sea Scrolls—offer an All-America team. Usually it's made up of paper pulp heroes picked by us near-sighted typewriter jockeys who sit so far from the field the only thing we can be sure of is the sex of the players.

I would like herewith to offer the Murray All-America. It will never make the Ed Sullivan Show or have its picture on bubblegum cards because its heroics were behind the scenes; its service to football, so to speak, invisible. May I present the sportsmen of the year:

*Pudge Butterfinger:* This mortal end set a school record by dropping 15 straight passes. The old record of 14 was set by Clumsy Brickle, but was thrown out by the district attorney, who found out it was on purpose. Turned out to be gamblers gave him a bigger Cadillac than the alumni.

*Ernest Sapp* is the team physiotherapist who

stopped 727 nosebleeds. In simple cases he did it with a clothespin, but if hemorrhage persisted, he tied off an artery. Gangrene set in, but by then the team had won the AP poll anyway; so it didn't matter. He also served by getting a wholesale rate on pep pills, and, after doling them out, also helped pull the boys down from the ceiling.

*Hamlet McGee* is the college press agent who got Earl Bedsore on the *Rock* magazine All-America on the basis of one good practice in September. This did not quite match the feat of his predecessor, Henry Wadsworth Shrimp, who got Butch Dropall on the 1960 *Rock* team in 1959. The magazine didn't want his statistics at press time; they just wanted to know if he was alive. The magazine's 1965 team will be locked on the presses this weekend and will include Ham's brother-in-law, who is still in high school unless the faculty discovers he sewed his school letter on upside down. Not from eccentricity but from illiteracy. He can add two and two all right, but he gets a different answer every time.

*William Jennings Weepeasy* is kept on the coaching staff for his inspirational speeches. He doesn't know much football but he has an entire family addicted to hepatitis, and his tearful pleas to "Win one for Aunt Maude" are so moving that the coaches have taken out insurance against an easy cure for the disease.

*Dr. Fall Guy* is the Dean of Admissions who not only accredited the entire first-string line, but had vines strung along the campus so they could swing from class to class. "Anthropoids are anthropoids," he claims. "Not everybody knows how to eat with a knife and fork." Dr. Guy is known to every college board in the country as the "Dean of Omissions." This award is posthumous. He was teaching the line table manners one night, but they ate him with their fingers anyway.

*Doc Cough* reset 827 bones during the season and got so proficient at it the team didn't have to call time out unless the fracture was multiple. He also set new standards in the use of novocaine, which he applied so liberally the starting backfield was able to play a whole game with only two sound legs among them.

*Rudyard Doap* is the water boy and lockerroom attendant who drowned trying to fix a leak in the whirlpool bath. It has been estimated he carried more water than the streets of Venice. His beanie cap—with the propeller still on it—will be retired in a bottle of sparkling water.

*Coach Cheatum N. Clip* revolutionized the game by stashing a star end in the band's tuba near the end of the half and having the winning TD pass thrown to him as the band was waiting in the end zone for the clumsy athletes to leave the field. He also dressed a halfback as a pompon girl one year, but the halfback was discovered when he smiled; the safetyman knew girl cheerleaders had more teeth than that. Coach Clip im-

proved the musical ear of every linebacker in the country. Linebackers knew that when the tuba hit a flat note they had to cover it.

& &

&

# IV.

# Fore

# Fun

# And

# Four-Forty

### SILENCE IS GOL-DARN

The two confirmed golf rivals, Doc and Jack, argued so consistently that they finally agreed not to talk at all during a match.

All went smoothly and silently until the sixteenth hole. There Doc walked up to a ball on the edge of the green, while Jack climbed into a sand trap.

Jack took one swing, then another, and another, and still another. Finally he topped a shot clear across the green and into a trap on the other

& &

&

side. From there he whanged the ball back into the first trap.

As he wearily recrossed the green, Doc broke the long silence.

"May I say a word?" he asked.

"Well," snarled Jack, "what is it?

"You're playing my ball," Doc replied.

**QUICK THINKING**

The two golfers were playing their first round together. The first one stepped to the tee, took a mighty swing, and put the ball right into the cup for a hole in one!

The other fellow nonchalantly stepped to the tee and said:

"Very nice. Now I'll take my practice swing before we start the game."

**COURSE FELLOW**

The duffer was brought into the hospital suffering from sunstroke. As the nurse began reading his temperature, "102–103–104," the suffering sportsman raised his head:

"Sweetie," he whispered, "what's par for this hospital?"

**SPIRIT OF '76**

The stuck-up society dame walked away from the eighteenth hole, her nose high in the air, and announced:

"I went around in 76."

To which a rival coldly answered:

"With Paul Revere, no doubt."

**BROTHERS UNDER THE SKIN**

Teeing off on the first hole, the duffer sliced his ball over a retaining wall way off to his right. He stared unbelievingly for a moment, then expressed himself fulsomely. As he moved off to his cart, he noticed a clergyman nearby. He immediately apologized for his language.

"That's all right, son," the clergyman said understandingly. "You have to let off steam once in a while."

"Sir," the duffer asked curiously, "how do you let off steam when you miss a shot?"

The clergyman smiled. "I just repeat the names of some of the members of my congregation—with feeling."

**AGONIZING PAYNE**

Having had to grow a beard for a Western, actor John

Payne essayed a round of golf on the toughest course in town. He eventually drove a ball into a trap and began futilely—and profanely—blasting away.

A fellow actor, on an adjoining fairway, came over to investigate the shocking sounds. He perceived John blasting away, with his whiskers flapping in the breeze.

"Good heavens, Payne," he gasped. "How long have you been in this trap?"

**A STICK IN TIME**

The duffer teed the ball, swung lustily, and watched with joy as a small object leaped away at a 45-degree angle.

"Thank goodness it's gone at last," he sighed.

"Mister," the caddie sighed, "that's your wristwatch."

**A REAL SPORT**

The man tore angrily out of the path beside the rough on the seventeenth hole, ran up to the Englishman, and shouted:

"You blundering idiot! You almost hit my wife just then."

"Oh, I say, I *am* sorry," replied the Englishman. "Have a shot at mine."

**CONSTANT GRIPPER**

Having apparently recovered from an attack of grippe, the weekend golf fanatic was all set to go out Sunday, when he suffered a relapse.

"Why can't you play this time?" grumbled his steady partner.

"Let me put it this way," he sadly answered. "My trouble is an overlapping grippe."

### WHAT'S NUDE?

The most believable golf story of the century was unwittingly supplied by the sports page of a Daytona Beach newspaper. It read:

> **At this point in the match, the gallery deserted the defending champion to swarm after Miss Blank, whose shorts were dropping on the green with astonishing regularity.**

### TEASE FOR TWO

Ralph Guglielmi, the former pro quarterback, is a bright fellow with a sharp sense of humor. His buddies are always kidding him about his golf game. Though he didn't start playing until his soph year in high school, he now shoots in the 70's.

One day Frank Gifford was giving him the needle about being a golf hustler.

"I'll play you for money," Frank teased. "But first tell me: What's your handicap?"

"Being Italian," Googs drawled.

### DUFFER'S DILEMMA

"That caddie kept laughing and laughing at me," the despondent duffer told his wife.

"You should have knocked his head off," the wife snapped.

"I would have, dear, but I didn't know what club to use."

**THE OLD-EN RULE**

Fred Perry, the great tennis star, fancied himself a golfer. Playing with Ellie Vines one afternoon, he couldn't do anything right. His game went from bad to disastrous. At the fourteenth hole, he exploded.

"You dumb little blighter!" he raged at his caddy. "What good are you? All you've done is carry the bag. Not once have you opened your silly mouth! Just tell me what club to use, just once! Let me hear you say something. Speak up! Tell me what to use!"

The caddy regarded Perry in silence for a moment, then he spoke:

"Mister, you asked me what to use. Use an old ball—a real old ball."

**A SIX ORGY**

The duffer finally smote a drive within distance of the green and eagerly turned to his caddy.

"Do you think I can reach it with a six?"

The diplomatic bag-toter nodded his head gravely.

"If you hit it often enough, sir."

**WHEN FORE IS A CROWD**

Hubby was a golf nut, wifey was bugged on auction sales, and both talked in their sleep. In the middle of the night, he would yell "Fore!" and she would respond with "Four-and-a-quarter!"

**SOMETHING IN ADVANCE**

The duffer had taken lessons from fifty pros over a period of five years, and still couldn't break 150. "I can't understand it," he complained in the lockerroom one day.

"Despite all the lessons, I played worse last year than the year before, and the year before it was worse than the year before that."

"How are you doing now?" asked a friend.

"You shouldn't have asked," was the reply. "Already I'm playing next year's game."

**WES OF THE GREAT DIVIDE**

Red Smith on the unfrocking of Wes Santee:

> **It seems generally agreed that the AAU has mishandled the case with a bumbling, ponderous ineptitude unmatched this side of Puerto Rico where, Conn McCreary reports, there is a jockey who boasts with pardonable pride that he has been ruled off for life thirteen times.**

**AVERY MAN HAS A BREAKING POINT**

Possibly the most absurd edict in the history of amateur sport was that blockbuster by good old Avery Brundage—barring from competition in the Olympics anyone who ever so much as *thought* of turning pro one day.

Jim Murray, the tiger of Los Angeles, put Avery's ukase into proper perspective with this barbed arrow:

**Avery's law will limit competition to members of the Rockefeller family and people on permanent relief, but this is the kind of heroic gesture needed to preserve the amateur image in America.**

**If a fellow wins a 100-meter dash and later cashes in on his Olympic fame by accepting a job as garbage collector, he will be called on to refund his medals, Olympic sweatsuit, and to write a letter of apology to Pincus Sober. "We are not conducting the Olympic Games as a training ground for garbage collectors," the committee will announce.**

### BAR AND GRILL

Before coming to the United States for a series of three meets, Valery Brumel reportedly cleared 7–4½ from a dirt takeoff in Leningrad.

"Were you surprised to clear that height?" one of the brilliant New York sportswriters asked Brumel the day before his first American meet.

"I wasn't surprised," Brumel courteously replied.

"How much over the bar were you when you cleared it?"

Brumel smiled faintly, and replied, "I had no time to look."

### SWEET SNELL OF SUCCESS

Peter Snell, one of the world's greatest distance runners, was a fabulous athlete in high school. One afternoon, after winning the interschool singles and doubles tennis titles in the morning and playing on the school's cricket team in the afternoon, he began working out on the track.

The school's headmaster happened to be passing, and stopped to watch Peter go around and around in the fading twilight.

Finally he called, "What are you doing now, Snell?"

"Oh, sir," was the polite reply, "I'm trying to keep fit."

### AMATEUR BANKERS

Probably the greatest distance runner of all time, Paavo Nurmi was distinguished for his amazing heartbeat, a flat 40, and his astonishing business acumen. He made more money out of amateur track than anyone before or since his celebrated tour of America in 1925. As one writer said of him:

"Paavo has the lowest heartbeat and the highest asking price of any runner in the world."

After Nurmi came Sonja Henie. Here's the way John Lardner described Sonja's first tour of America:

"Sonja Henie went up and down the country with a pair of skates and a vacuum cleaner, picking up whatever money Nurmi had overlooked."

### THE LOONINESS OF THE LONG-DISTANCE RUNNER

The track squad at Wakefield High School, Arlington, Virginia, got such a boot out of the following essay that Coach Julian U. Stein felt compelled to relay it to us. Entitled "Mental Attitude in Cross-Country," it was written by Bill Bernard, a former Wakefield harrier.

***Runners take your marks* . . . Relax Bernard; you have two miles to go.**

*Now, set* . . . Just two miles; you can run it in less than 11:30.

*Go* . . . Two miles! I'll never make it. I shouldn't have gone to that party last night; it wasn't over till 11:00; I didn't get home till 3:00; four hours sleep. The pace is way too fast. Why don't they slow down? They can't keep this pace up for two miles.

*One-quarter mile (. . . :88, :89, :90)* . . . I should have stayed home today. I should have said I was sick or something.

*One-half mile* . . . My leg hurts; Coach should have taped it. I'll have to drop out if it gets worse. I have a terrible stitch, too.

*Three-quarter mile* . . . I have to hurdle that chain. Maybe I'll trip and be able to quit. If I limp, maybe Coach will notice and take me out.

*One mile (5:48, 5:49)* . . . Pick it up, Bill. (5:50 . . .)

*One and one-quarter miles* . . . Baker's passing me. Why did I ever go out for cross-country? I'm no good; haven't a chance of breaking 11:30 now. Why don't I quit? I'll just walk up to Coach and tell him . . . McClinton's passing me! He can't do that! Fight him off; check out.

*One and one-half miles* . . . There's the finish; don't fag now, Bernard. What does McClinton think he's doing? He's running faster! So is Jerry. I can't let him pass me now. Pick it up, Bernard. 100 yards to go—SPRINT, damn you, SPRINT!

*Two miles (11:08, 11:09, 11:10)* . . . Impossible! Jack, bring me my sweatsuit, will you please? Thanks.

**You know, what Coach said is right—the deciding factor in cross-country is mental attitude!**

. . . AND A 2, 3, 4

Dick Calisch, track coach at Prospect High School (Mt. Prospect, Ill.), is also a poet, and, judging from the following contribution, "High Hurdles," a pretty darned good one. The meter cleverly jibes with the footfalls of a hurdles race, the rhyming word always coming at the hurdles.

*The pistol-flash*
*and off they*
*dash*
*as lithe and*
*fast*
*as breezes*
*blast*
*a leaf a-*
*long.*
*No tune or*
*song*
*goes quite as*
*strong*
*or near as*
*true*
*as hurdles*
*do,*
*and all too*
*few*
*can dance the*
*tune*
*that hurdlers do in the afternoon.*

**POLE CAT**

Modern pole vaulting through the eyes of Dick Young, crack New York columnist (and calumnist):

> **Do you think the offense has passed the defense in pole vaulting? The whole thing is really a fraud, of course: this business about John Pannel clearing 17 feet with the catapult pole. The genuine record holders are the Zacchini Family who, every day during circus week, get shot out of a cannon clear across Madison Square Garden. There's only one way to make the pole vault a spot again. Seat a midget on the crossbar with a mace, and have him swing at anybody trying to clear it.**

& &

&

# V. Catches In The Wry

### JIMMY'S BALLISTIC MISSILE-TOE

Our favorite coach, Jimmy Dykes, fractured the banquet circle with a discourse on his travails as a manager at Baltimore. All season long one of the owners kept second-guessing him, making life unbearable. One day the owner came into the dressing room and started berating Jimmy for all the things he was doing wrong.

Just before the game was about to begin, Dykes turned and started leaving the room.

& &

&

"Jimmy," the voice nagged, "even your uniform is dirty. Why don't you get the grass off the back of your pants?"

Dykes turned and stared at the nag. "That's not grass," he murmured, "it's mistletoe."

**AT HOME AND A BROAD**

Before the traditional double-header on a brutally hot Fourth of July, the bosomy soprano from the local opera company took her place at the plate to sing, "The Star-Spangled Banner."

Everybody stood up, of course, then sat down after she finished the first verse. But she promptly launched into the second verse. Up came the crowd again, and down it went again after she had finished the last line. But there she still stood. As she raised her voice to start the third verse, a hard-bitten bleacherite bawled:

"Why don't somebody give that broad a base on balls?"

**NO PLACE FOR ASTRONAUTS**

As the space capsule of Astronaut Walter Schirra was making its dramatic re-entry into the earth's atmosphere, the *Dodgers* were kicking and fumbling the ball around in their last playoff game with the *Giants.*

"It's a good thing that Schirra wasn't dropped at Chavez Ravine," mused one of the writers. "Nobody would have picked him up."

**HEAVENLY RICHES**

Stan Musial was showing a group of friends around St. Louis. He showed them his restaurant, his bowling alley, some of his real estate holdings, and then the bank of which he's a board member. On the drive back to the hotel, the car passed St. Gabriel's Church in Musial's parish.

"They're holding Adorations," said The Man. "Let's stop in."

As the party started up the wide stone steps of the church, one of Stan's friends turned to him and said, "Hey, Musial, do you own a piece of this place, too?"

**THE KING'S ENGLISH**

The school teacher was voicing strong objections to Dizzy Dean's grammar. She said it was ruining the students in her class.

"It's disgraceful," she wrote. "How can the networks possibly permit you to appear in front of a microphone when you don't even know the King's English?"

Dean scribbled back:

"But I do know it, ma'am. And if you want to get technical about it, Ol' Diz also knows that the Queen is English."

### DARK-NESS AT NOON

As the *Giants* grudgingly yielded ground in the 1963 pennant race, Al Dark refused to concede the hopelessness of his position.

First he said, "If we can beat the *Dodgers* in 7 out of the 9 games we face them, we have a great chance."

The next time it was, "If we can beat the *Dodgers* 7 out of the 8 times we play 'em, we'll still be in the race."

Finally the point of no return was reached. The *Giants* lost to the *Dodgers* once more and were out of the race for good. Leonard Schechter of the New York *Post* commented on Dark's unique timetable in this fashion:

"By Dark's own reckoning, the *Giants* will have to win five of their remaining four games with the *Dodgers* to stay in contention."

### DUREN WORKING HOURS

Bill Rigney, fed up with Rhyne Duren's wildness, finally unloaded him on the *Phillies*. "Every time you warmed him up," explained Rig, "you had to warm up another pitcher with him. He was more expendable than dependable."

Though wild, Duren did have a scorching fast ball. Leon Wagner described it best:

"When Duren hits you in the side, the ball doesn't come out."

**A DOUBTING THOMAS**

In 11 of his first 15 seasons in pro ball, Frank Thomas wound up in a cellar club. Which may account for the fact that, upon joining the *Mets*, he began reading *The Power of Positive Thinking*.

The big outfielder became excited about the book; he felt sure it would help him at the plate. Then one day he suddenly stopped reading it. His roommate, curious about Thomas's sudden disinterest, asked him about it.

"I was crazy about the book," Frank admitted. "I was sure it would help my hitting, until a thought occurred to me: What if the pitchers had read it, too? That's when I quit on it."

**AULD LANG SIGN**

After losing a tough game, Dizzy Dean blasted the umpires, casting aspersions not only on their eyesight but on their integrity as well. Hauled before Ford Frick, then president of the National League, Dean insisted he had been misquoted. Frick said he'd accept the explanation if Dean put it in writing.

Dean's face clouded. "Look here, Mr. Frick," he snapped. "I admit I was misquoted, but I ain't signin' nothin'."

**DONKEY SERENADE**

Back in Ray Blades's time, the *Cardinals* used to conduct two workouts a day in spring training while the *Yankees*, across town, worked out only once. The ineffable Pepper Martin, cognizant of the *Yankee* championship record, asked his manager if it wouldn't be wise to borrow the *Yankee* practice of just one workout a day.

"No," replied Blades, "to be like the *Yankees* we have to work twice as hard on our mistakes. Two workouts a day will do it."

Pepper thought this over for a moment, then drawled:

"You know, Skipper, I got a jackass back in Oklahoma, and you can work him from sunup till sundown and he ain't never going to win the Kentucky Derby."

**CASH ON THE LINE**

A spirit of unrest ran through the Detroit *Tigers* during the middle of the 1963 season. First, Manager Bob Sheffing was fired. Then his staff of coaches was released. Rumor had it that the trainer and the clubhouse boy would go next.

Upon hearing the rumor, first baseman Norm Cash shook his head.

"Too bad about the clubhouse boy," he said. "He was having a helluva year."

**A HORSE OF ANOTHER COLOR**

During the short, abortive life of the Continental League and the subsequent skulduggery connected with the expansion of the two big leagues, our big league owners hardly covered themselves with glory. Their cupidity and selfishness emerged clearly and pitifully—making them fair bait for the classic remark from Red Smith:

"When Gene Autry got the Los Angeles team, it was the first time a franchise had been acquired by a whole horse."

**A DROP KID BY UNCLE ROBBIE**

One of the most colorful and lovable managers of all

time, the late Wilbur Robinson always had a special spot in his heart for the equally colorful Babe Herman. The affection extended to Babe's six-year-old son.

So you can imagine the kid's confusion one day when, after climbing trustingly onto Uncle Robbie's ample lap, he was dumped unceremoniously onto the Ebbets Field turf. He looked up bewildered, to find an accusing finger pointing at him.

"Why," thundered Robbie, "ain't your old man hitting?"

### COMING THROUGH THE RYE

Here's a riddle for all you high domes:

If two gals fortify themselves with a bottle of firewater, hie themselves to the ball park, and become magnificently happy, what inning is it and how many men are on base?

Answer: It's the last of the fifth and the bags are loaded.

### HITTING BACK

When tough Early Wynn was a youthful fire-baller, his manager, Bucky Harris, decided to start him against the Yankees. The veteran Yankee outfielder, Ben Chapman, looked into the visitors' dugout on his way to the outfield.

"Hey, Bucky," he shouted, "I hear you're pitching that kid, Wynn. I figure to get five hits."

"If you get five hits," snarled Wynn, "you'll get the last four lying on your back."

### SEASON'S GREETINGS

It was the final day of the season and after the game everybody was going around wishing everyone a good winter.

But not tough Early Wynn. Shoving his head into the umpires' room, he growled:

"I hope you guys have a good winter. You sure had a lousy summer."

**BATS IN THE BASKET**

The fastest gun in baseball with a quip, Joe Garagiola rarely fails to connect with anything he swings at. Like when a waiter laid a basket of breadsticks on the speakers' table at a banquet. Joe took one quick look and quipped:

"I see that the Mets' bats have arrived."

**A MODEL FAILURE**

"You know how particular baseball players are about the model bats they select every year," Garagiola will tell you. "Well, whenever I asked for mine, the clubhouse boy would never ask what kind. He'd ask me what for."

**A HAND FOR PLUMBERS**

Most of the old-time catchers have fingers like weather-vanes, with gnarled fingers pointing in every direction. "When two old catchers meet on the street and shake hands," claims Garagiola, "it takes a plumber twenty minutes to pry them apart."

**BLUE DAZE**

"When you watch Joe Cunningham play the outfield," says Joe, "you begin to understand why the Blue Shield rates are so high."

**WISH YOU WEREN'T HERE**

One afternoon, when Garagiola was with the *Cardinals*, a *Pirate* pitcher named Rip Sewell tried to dust off Joe. Garagiola promptly laid the next pitch down the first-base line and tried to climb up Sewell's back with his spikes. But the pitcher throw a block at Joe that kicked him right into the *Pirates'* dugout.

"Next thing I knew," says Joe, "one *Pirate* had me by one leg, another by the other leg, and somebody was saying, 'Make a wish.' "

**CULTURAL EXCHANGE**

When Joe caught for the *Cardinals*, one of the pitchers was Jim Brosnan, now renowned as a best-selling author.

"I was never intellectual enough for Jim," declares Joe. "He's the only pitcher I ever knew who made a catcher feel uncomfortable. When you went out to talk to him, like to tell him the bases were loaded, the way he looked at you, you thought your zipper was open."

**THE AGE OF UNREASON**

Upon hearing that Dummy Hoy, the Stone Age outfielder (1888–1902) was going to throw out the first ball in the 1961 World Series, impish Joe exclaimed:

"They tell me Dummy Hoy is 99 years old. Is that his real or his baseball age?"

**PIZZA THE BALL**

When the Senate Monopoly Sub-Committee invited

him to Washington to testify on baseball, Garagiola, then catcher with the *Cubs*, first thought it was a gag. "I thought maybe the Italian consul in Washington had lost his recipe for pizza pie."

**CRUELEST CUT**

Garagiola was with the *Tigers* when Frank House signed for a $75,000 bonus. The first day of practice, House took six swings instead of the usual five. Garagiola promptly sneered, "Look, you got 75 grand and can't even count to five."

**GREAT DAY FOR THE IRISH**

Beans Reardon, the famous ump, once called Danny Murtaugh out on strikes, and the fiery Irishman blew his top, forcing Beansie to toss him out of the game. After going half-way to the dugout, Danny suddenly retraced his steps.

"Beansie," he said softly, "do you know what you've just done? Look around you. There's Furillo in right field, Amoros in left, Robinson on second, Lavagetto on third.

"Do you realize, Beansie, that when you threw me out, you left yourself the only Irishman on the field? You're all alone, Beansie, all alone."

**TIP FOR TAT**

The mighty Babe Ruth tried to stretch a double into a triple, but the third baseman had the ball waiting for him. Babe made a beautiful slide, but the umpire, Pants Rowland, shook his head.

"That was a fabulous slide, Babe," he said, "but you're out."

Babe got to his feet, walked over to the ump, and apparently exchanged a few words with him. Then he trotted into the *Yankee* dugout.

"What did you tell Rowland?" Manager Miller Huggins asked.

"Tell him?" repeated Babe. "I didn't say anything. I was just looking for a quarter to tip him for the compliment."

### "KNOWS" FOR NEWS

A rhubarb broke out in the seventh inning, and Jimmy Dykes—as usual—rushed onto the field. With three umpires around him, he stated his case and, as usual, lost. Walking back to the dugout, he spotted the fourth ump, Jocko Conlan, and appealed to him.

"But, Jimmy," said Jocko, "I don't even know what this is about."

Dykes pointed to the other umps. "Then join them. They don't know what it's all about either."

### POINT OF THE STORY

Jim Gentile was needling the *Orioles'* second-string catcher, Hank Foiles, a good-natured boy from the Deep South.

"Southerners don't move out of the South," Jim kidded. "If they did, nobody would understand them and they'd starve to death."

"I haven't missed too many meals," smiled Foiles.

"Well, you've learned to point, Hank," replied Gentile.

### RAINY DAY INSURANCE

After being presented with a plaque as the outstanding pitcher for 1961, Warren Spahn lugged it into Manager Birdie

Tebbetts's office and said, "Would you mind if I hung this up in here?"

"Go ahead," said the puzzled manager, "but why would you want to do that?"

"Because," said Spahn, "next time I have a bad day I want you to be reminded I can't be as lousy as I looked."

**HIGH AND DRY-SDALE**

At the time Don Drysdale was popping off about wanting to be traded from the *Dodgers,* Vice-President Buzzy Bavasi called the sulking pitcher on the phone. The phone rang several times before Don's wife, Ginger, answered.

"I'm sorry it took me so long to answer," she apologized. "I was bathing the baby."

"Which one?" Buzzy asked.

**BOAST ON TOAST**

All during the 1960 season, cocky Charlie Dressen kept predicting that his *Braves* would win the pennant. Solly Hemus, listening to Chuck one day, dryly remarked:

"Dressen is so worked up that if he doesn't watch out he'll finish five games ahead of the *Braves.*"

**SINKER OR SWIM**

Batting against Lew Burdette one night, Norm Larker became convinced that the *Braves'* pitcher was throwing spitters. "C'mon, Frank," he complained to Umpire Secory, "the guy's throwing spitters."

"Naah," replied Secory, "them were sinkers."

"Sinkers!" snapped Larker. "One of them 'sinkers' just splashed me in the right eye!"

**STATUE OF LIMITATIONS**

Livewire Earl Battey, *Twins'* catcher, noticed a teammate goofing off in infield practice.

"Hey, man, start moving around," Battey yelled. "You've been standing around so long, they're going to make a ground rule out of you."

**SORE-TAINLY**

Red Ruffing, the pitching coach, was lecturing on how modern pitchers pamper their arms.

"Why, when I was with the *Yankees*," he said, "I'd wait one day after pitching and then go out in the outfield and start throwing to the plate."

"Didn't your arm ever get sore?" a reporter asked.

"Always," Ruffing replied.

**PLANE SPEAKING**

Danny Murtaugh's wife, Kate, wore a new hat all during the three 1960 World Series games played in New York. Returning to Pittsburgh by plane, she sat under an air vent which kept blowing the feathers on the hat in all directions.

Harvey Haddix finally sent word to her:

"Tell Mrs. Murtaugh if that hat moves again I'm going to take aim at it with a rifle."

**HATCH OFF TO JOE**

Moose Skowron whacked the ball down the right-field line, and Rocky Colavito made a great try for it. He took a long sitting slide, but just missed the ball. As luck would have it, he landed on the ball and couldn't find it. Everyone in the park—except Rocky—knew he was sitting on it.

In front of the *Indian* dugout, screaming like a lunatic, was Manager Joe Gordon.

"For heaven's sake," he kept yelling, "somebody tell him to get off the ball before he hatches it."

### BROTHERLY LOVE

Mickey Owen and Walker Cooper had quite a brawl in St. Louis one afternoon. The first time Mickey came up to bat the next day, he turned to Cooper, who was working behind the plate.

"How about shaking hands, Coop?" he asked.

"Sure, Mickey," replied the *Cardinal* catcher, and they shook.

Owen then turned to face the slants of Cooper's brother, Mort—and fanned on three straight pitches. As Mickey started for the dugout, Walker couldn't resist a dig.

"Hey, Mick," he shouted, "don't you want to shake hands with my brother, too?"

### DRESSEN DOWN

Manager Charlie Dressen had removed the famous screwball, Frank Gabler, from the mound, and the Great Gabbo's pride was injured. Stripping off his shirt, flexing his mighty muscles and pounding his chest, Gabler pleaded:

"Look, Charlie, I'm in great shape. I never felt better."

"Look, Gab," replied Dressen, "I don't want you to fight anyone for me. I just want you to get somebody out."

**IN A MINORS KEY**

When Roy Hartsfield and Augie Donatelli were in the minors together, the former as an infielder and the latter as an ump, they got into an argument over a call.

"Roy," said Little Augie, "if you ever learned to hit that pitch, you'd make the big leagues."

"And if you ever learned how to call it right, we could go on the same train," retorted Hartsfield.

**MAKE BELIEVE**

When Babe Herman, the great-hit no-field *Dodger* hero, heard that someone was making the rounds of the night clubs, stores, and the like impersonating him, he devised a plan for catching the rascal.

"Next time anyone comes around claiming he's Babe Herman," he advised, "take him outside and fungo a fly ball to him. If he catches it, call the cops."

**HEAR, HEAR**

In his first two years with the *Indians,* Herb Score threw just about as fast as anyone who ever lived. One day Roy Sievers stepped in against him, and it was *buzz, buzz, buzz*—three quick strikes. Roy strolled to the dugout, politely put his bat into the rack, and sat down.

"He threw me the radio ball," he announced.

"Radio ball?" asked Chuck Stobbs.

"That's right," said Sievers. "You can hear it, but you can't see it."

**IT MAKES NO CENSUS**

Vinegar Bend Mizell takes a lot of ribbing about his Alabama home town. But he has a ready answer to the most common question:

"What's the population of Vinegar Bend?"

"It's either 117 or 119," he replies. "Two people went off into the woods a couple of months ago, and we don't know yet whether they're coming back."

**WHERE THERE'S A WILL-IAMS**

Watching Dick Stuart bashing the ball for fantastic distances and then butchering the easiest kind of ground balls at first base, a press box wit sighed:

"He's a Williams-type player: he bats like Ted and fields like Esther."

**YES, SIR,
THAT'S MY BABY**

The Baltimore *Orioles* have so many young pitchers that whenever Coach Luman Harris comes out to make a replacement, the fans start chanting:

"Here comes the baby sitter!"

**BLOWING TAPS**

Don Blasingame was at bat one night and grew increasingly annoyed at Umpire Frank Dascoli. When the ump called "Strike three!" on a high, hard one, Don blew his top.

"Listen, Frank," he snapped, "how can you sleep with the lights on?"

**HEADED FOR THE PASS**

The fact that Mickey Mantle receives so many intentional passes is a source of heated debate. A lot of experts feel that walking Mickey intentionally makes no sense. After all, the *Yankee* bomber can't clout a homer every time up.

Roger Maris is on the pitcher's side. "I think it's smarter to give the big man four balls for one base than one ball for four bases."

**NO SOAP**

When the blunderful *Phillies* played in Shibe Park, there was a sign on the rightfield fence which read:

THE PHILLIES USE LIFEBUOY SOAP

The day after losing their fifteenth straight, the *Phillies* came out on the field and found that during the night someone had painted on the sign:

AND THEY STILL STINK

**HOP, FAITH AND CHARITY**

The weird hops on the concrete surface of Forbes Field give everyone a headache—the writers as well as the players. One day Bob Friend chopped one in front of the plate and made first before the ball came down into the pitcher's glove. Bill Virdon came up next and hoisted a 450-foot fly to the center fielder.

One of the reporters, who had been typing, looked up just in time to see the fielder catch the ball against the fence. "I didn't see the ball hit, fellers," he yawned. "Was it a fly ball, or did it bounce?"

**COLLEGE BOY**

In the *Yankee* batting cage, pitcher Zack Monroe took three swings instead of two, drawing the attention of Yogi Berra.

"Hey, you," yelled Yogi. "Doncha know how to count? You ever go to school?"

It just happens that Monroe is an honor graduate of Bradley University. When this fact was brought to Yogi's attention, he snapped:

"So what? I was in Harvard myself once."

"In a jar?" politely asked Mickey Mantle.

**ONLY IN AMERICA**

When Robert Briscoe, Mayor of Dublin, visited the United States, Yogi was told that Briscoe was the first Jewish mayor in Dublin history.

"Isn't that wonderful!" Yogi exclaimed. "It could happen only in America."

**QUICK AS A BUNNING**

Yogi's habit of rapping bad pitches for good hits dazed the experts. One of them once asked Jim Bunning how he pitched to the *Yankee* catcher.

"With a lump in my throat," muttered the right-hander.

**DRAW PLAY**

Joe Garagiola was sitting around swapping small talk with Yogi, and the conversation drifted to the attendance problem at Kansas City.

"The *Athletics* can't seem to draw at home," observed Garagiola.

Yogi nodded his head wisely.

"If the fans don't want to come out," he said, "nobody can stop them."

**UPON SECOND THOUGHT**

Yogi Berra's teammates love to make up stories about him. Mickey Mantle swears that he and Yogi were taking a walk one day when they were horrified to see a baby topple off the roof of a nearby three-family house. Yogi, with his quick reflexes, dashed over in an instant and made a miraculous catch.

But force of habit took over. He straightened up and threw the baby to second base.

**DOUBLE X**

The first time Jimmy Piersall came up to the plate in Yankee Stadium, he went through his usual mannerisms—crossing himself and then drawing an x in the dirt with his bat.

Yogi Berra promptly stepped in front of Piersall, crossed himself, and said, "Now what are you gonna do, Jimmy?"

**AN "A" FOR EF-FORD**

Whitey Ford has a rollicking sense of humor and a good sense of proportion. Both stood him in good stead when he heard that the fans were going to give him a day.

"Are you excited about it, Whitey?" asked a sportswriter.

"Are you kidding?" Whitey replied. "I've been campaigning for a day so long I'm afraid I'll get a 1953 automobile."

**STUNTING ON DEFENSE**

Whitey can come through with a fast one on every occasion. One afternoon, after he had given up a homer to a .220 hitter, his catcher, Elston Howard, walked out to the mound with an unhappy look on his face.

Before Elston could put in a word, Ford shook his head. "Ellie," he said, "Choo Choo Coleman would never have called that pitch."

**A TIME FOR UPHEAVAL**

After clinching the 1960 pennant in Boston, the *Yankees* entrained for Washington. Spud Murphy, their batting-practice pitcher, came up with a stomach upset.

"Hey," shouted Yogi Berra to Whitey Ford, "look at Murphy; he heaved—"

"Yeah," said Whitey, "that's the best stuff he's had all year."

**WATCH THE FORD GO BY-BY**

Whitey Ford was in a jam. Chuck Cottier was at bat with the bases full. Manager Ralph Houk walked out for a conference.

"How do you feel?" he asked.

"I'm all right," replied the great left-hander. "Cottier's up and I won't have any trouble with him."

Houk walked back to the dugout, but before he could sit down he heard the crack of the bat. Cottier had hit Whitey's first pitch out of the park, and the game was over.

Ford came storming into the dugout and slammed his glove down on the bench.

"That guy Cottier!" he raged. "If he'd hit the ball right, it would have gone foul!"

**AN OLE MISS IS AS GOOD AS A MILE**

Soon after Jake Gibbs arrived at Yankee Stadium, Whitey Ford took a phone call for him.

"Hey, Jake," he called, "it's for you. Your coach at Ole Miss says you forgot to pay income tax for your last two years there."

**COMPARISON SHOPPING**

In the midst of that 16–3 trouncing the *Yankees* gave the *Pirates* in the third game of the 1960 World Series, Gino Cimoli, coming to the plate, said to the *Yankees'* catcher, Elston Howard:

"You guys better watch out. You're not that good."

"Gino, you're right," replied Ellie. "We're not that good. You fellows just make us look that way."

**FLIGHT FRIGHT**

On a wind-swept night, John Carmichael, the Chicago columnist, bumped into Bob Feller at an airport.

"John!" shouted Feller, then the greatest name in baseball. "I hope we're on the same flight."

"If we were," Carmichael replied, gazing fearfully at the heavens, "I'd cancel. Do you think I want to go down on the same plane with Bob Feller? I want an obituary of my own. I owe it to my family."

**HALE, HALE MAURY WILLS**

Dodger shortstop Maury Wills panicked his teammates in spring training. While leading them through calisthenics, he gave his orders as follows:

"Okay, now everyone inhale and [pause] dehale."

**HAND TROUBLE**

Gordy Coleman and Gene Freese supplied a lot of home-run power to the Cincinnati pennant drive in 1961. But neither shone in the field. The fact that they were roomies was something of a team joke.

"It's no use calling their room," Jim Brosnan told a reporter. "Both of them have such bad hands they wouldn't be able to pick up the phone."

**FEUD FOR THOUGHT**

Frankie Frisch had a mock feud with Casey Stengel. One day Casey, stepping off a curb, was struck by a taxicab and suffered a broken leg.

The first telegram to reach him at the hospital was from Frisch. It read:

YOUR UNSUCCESSFUL ATTEMPT TO COMMIT SUICIDE DEEPLY LAMENTED

**SKEWERED PREXY ON TOAST**

When Will Harridge was the do-nothing president of

the American League, a midwestern sports columnist devastated him with this telling shot:

"An empty taxicab pulled up in front of the hotel here today and out of it stepped Will Harridge."

**FRICK-ASEE À LA PARKER**

Baseball Commissioner Ford Frick was a hard-working baseball writer before donning the ermine. Moved by the muse often, he would lapse into rather mediocre poetry. It was Dan Parker who administered the coup de grace to Frick's predilection for iambic pentameter.

"Ford Frick has never been mentioned for poet laureate," Dan wrote, "not even of Bulgaria."

**SIGN OF THE TIMES**

Baseball scouts aren't easily flustered. They've seen and heard everything. But Houston scout John Breen really came a cropper last winter when a young prospect told him:

"No sir, I ain't ready to sign a contract yet, but if you got some bonus money on you I'll sign a verbal agreement."

**NO KNOW-WHAT**

*Giant* coach Wes Westrum hit the horsehide right on the head in a discussion of baseball as the fans see it:

"It's like church. Many attend, but few understand."

**IN A LITTLE SPANISH TOWN**

Late in the 1961 season, after Roger Maris had belted

his fifty-ninth homer, two teenage girls dropped in on the *Yankees'* hotel in Baltimore. Earl Torgeson, who was rooming with Luis Arroyo, ran into them in the hall. The girls grabbed the *Yankee* coach and demanded to see Roger Maris.

"All we want to do is shake his hand," they pleaded.

"We know he's in that room," one of the girls said.

"No he isn't," replied Torgeson.

"We know he is," the girls cried. "Please knock on the door."

So Torgy knocked on the door and said, "Rog, you in there?"

"Si, si," came the answer, "and I theenk I heet my seextieth home run mañana."

**WHAT A RELIEF**

Luis Arroyo bailed out Whitey Ford so often during the 1961 season that the Ford-Arroyo team became something of a joke. *Red Sox* wit Joe Ginsberg topped 'em all with this one:

"I hear that at all the banquets this winter Ford will speak for seven minutes and Arroyo for two."

**SALARY TONIC**

The famous *White Sox* pitcher, Hollis (Sloppy) Thurston, once won twenty games, but the team wound up in the cellar anyhow. At contract time, Sloppy wrote a letter asking for a wage increase.

"Don't forget," he wrote, "I won twenty games for a last-place club."

He received his answer by telegram:

NO RAISE. WE COULD HAVE FINISHED LAST WITHOUT YOU.

**TIME MARCHES ON**

The *White Sox* brought up a 17-year-old bonus baby from a little town in Arkansas. Manager Al Lopez sat the kid next to him on the bench so that he could point out some of the finer points of the game.

In the second inning, Nellie Fox drew a base on balls. When the next batter lined a hit down the right-field line, Nellie correctly wheeled around second and went on to third—only to be cut down by a beautiful throw from Roger Maris.

Lopez turned to the kid and said, "He was right to try for third. You won't see another throw like that in a hundred years."

In the seventh inning with Fox again on first, the same batter lined to the same spot and the same outfielder cut down Fox trying for third.

The kid on the bench tapped Manager Lopez on the shoulder. "Mistah Lopez," he said wonderingly, "time sure does fly heah in the Nohth!"

**IT'S AILMENT-ARY, DEAR WATSON**

The young pitcher, a confirmed hypochondriac, complained so much about his condition that the manager sent him to a psychiatrist. Like many hypochondriacs, the boy had done extensive reading on muscle spasms, and he mentioned a rare muscular disorder as the root of his difficulty.

"Come, come, now," protested the psychiatrist, "you wouldn't know whether you had that or not. With that ailment there's no discomfort of any kind."

"I know," moaned the pitcher, "my symptoms exactly."

**INDIAN GIVER**

The manager sought out his second baseman in the lockerroom.

"Billy," he said, "remember all those batting tips, double-play pivots, the base-running hints I gave you this afternoon?"

"Sure, skipper," enthused the player.

"Forget 'em," murmured the manager. "We just traded you to Kansas City."

**A BO FOR ALL SEASONS**

When Bo Belinsky was having his great year in the night-club-and-romance league, columnist Bob Sylvester commented:

"I hope baseball doesn't shorten Bo Belinsky's career."

**STUDY IN BROWNS**

When Bill Veeck bought the hapless St. Louis *Browns* in 1951—a team that had made the first division only eleven times in 47 years—he caught at least one sports columnist off base.

"Many critics were surprised to know the *Browns* could be bought," wrote John Lardner, "because they didn't know that the *Browns* were owned."

**SING ALONG WITH GENE**

Now that Gene Autry is a big-league club owner, sports

columnist Dick Young can envisage him at future American League summit meetings, getting up and saying:

"Gentlemen, I'm going to vote on this matter, but first let me sing you a little song."

**THE OPERATION WAS A SUCCESS, BUT . . .**

Pete Reiser, Dodger coach:

"Frank Howard had a tough time learning the strike zone. We worked and worked on it, and we now got him to lay off the pitches a shade outside or a shade high—the sort he used to drive out of the park."

**KELL-JOY**

When George Kell broke in with the *Athletics,* Bobo Newsom was in the twilight of his pitching career.

In a tight game one afternoon, the *Tigers* had a man on first and none out. With every pitch by Newsom, Kell would charge in for a bunt. Finally, with the count three and one, Bobo called for time and motioned Kell to the mound.

"What are you trying to do to me?" he growled.

"What do you mean?" Kell stammered. "I'm supposed to break down the line on your pitch, aren't I?"

"'Yeah," snapped Newsom, "but you're getting to the plate faster than my fast ball. You're making me look bad."

**FEATHER DUSTER**

Bobo never hesitated to keep the batters uneasy and shaky up at the plate.

"Did you ever deliberately knock anyone down?" he was asked.

"No, I never did," he grinned. "But I recollect that the ball did."

**AFTER THE BRAWL WAS OVER**

A fellow in a box seat caught a foul ball. The fellow in the next seat asked him whether he could see the ball. The ball was passed over, carefully inspected, then thrown back to the playing field. The foul-catcher blew his stack. He emptied a beer into the other fellow's face, and before you knew it all eight occupants of the box were busily flinging punches. The special officers rushed to the scene and evicted all eight.

"That's a helluva note," snarled the fellow who had caught the ball. "All eight of us get tossed out, but the darned ball stays in the game."

**A SMASH ENDING**

Some years back the *Athletics* and the *Senators* staged a battle royal in the middle of the diamond. While Umpire Cal Hubbard scurried about knocking heads together to foment peace, the biggest and toughest of the ball-players, Bob Johnson, stood on the fringe of the melee with a big grin on his face.

The last man out of the dugout was Joe Krakauskas, the fast, wild, and unpronounceable *Senator* pitcher. As Joe wound up and started to take a punch at the *Athletics'* little shortstop, Skeeter Newsome, a hand grabbed him by the shoulder and a fist crashed against his jaw. He dropped like a shot quail, lay still for a moment, then arose and scrambled back to the dugout. Later on he explained that he thought Cal Hubbard had smashed him.

The next afternoon a reporter approached Bob Johnson. "You weren't having any of that fight, Bob," he said, "so why did you clobber poor Joe like that?"

"Because," Johnson answered, "I never could hit that so-and-so when he was pitching."

**SHIFTY ADDITION**

Bob Uecker, utility catcher for the *Braves*, was bragging about his roomie, Eddie Mathews.

"I think it's worth noting," he said, "that between the two of us we've hit 420 home runs."

"That can't be," a teammate remarked.

"'Look it up," said Uecker. "Eddie has hit 419 homers and I've hit one."

**MAN-SIZED MISS**

Little Albie Pearson, the smallest player in the majors, leaped high for a long fly ball, only to see it soar over his head into the bleachers. Upon returning to the dugout after the inning, he turned to Manager Bill Rigney.

"Did I miss the ball by much?" he inquired.

"No, Albie," replied Rigney. "You just missed by a man."

**A SOCK WITH A RUN-IN**

In the bottom of the tenth inning, Mickey Mantle caught one of Bill Fischer's fast balls and came within a foot of becoming the first batter in history to drive a fair ball out of Yankee Stadium.

The titanic swat broke up the ball game and awed

everyone. Even Fischer was able to kid about it in the dressing room.

"I could tell how far the ball was going," he told the reporters, "by the way all my outfielders started running in."

**HOW NOW, BROWN COW?**

As a pre-game gimmick in Baltimore, infielder Bob Johnson took on pitcher Mike McCormick in a cow-milking contest. Johnson tugged and strained. McCormick pulled and prayed.

Finally the drops began to fall. A considerable time later, a huffing and puffing McCormick was declared the winner.

Accepting his prize, McCormick said modestly:

"I never could have done it without the cow."

**CORN ON THE KOBS**

John Kobs, Michigan State baseball coach, was rendered speechless only once in his life. Having been victimized by some extremely questionable umpiring, he went into the umpires' dressing quarters and bitterly complained.

Whereupon one of the arbiters tartly answered, "Oh, you're just mad because we beat you."

**WHAT A METS**

The New York *Mets* are worthy heirs to the old Brooklyn *Dodgers*. Formed in 1962, they're a pretty hopeless collection of has-beens, never-wases, and grass-green rookies. But, like the *Dodgers*, they have a loud and loyal group of fans, and funny things always seem to be happening to them.

One day they were practicing fielding bunts. The pitcher and first baseman were charging the ball, and the catcher, Joe Ginsberg, kept shouting what base to throw to.

On the first bunt, Ginsberg yelled to Hodges, "Third! Third!" On the next play, he yelled, "First! First!" On the third play, Ginsberg, now a bit tired but eager as ever, yelled, "Thirst! Thirst!"

**STOLEN BASE**

After losing a couple of games on bone-head plays, Marv Throneberry became a target for a loud chorus of razzberries every time he came up. His unpopularity became a joke as the season wore on. Even Marvelous Marv entered into the spirit of the thing.

He was sitting on the bench one night when Ed Bouchee made a costly error, then struck out with the tying run on base. The *Mets* fans gave Ed the bazzoo as he plodded back to the bench. There he was greeted by Marv:

"What are you trying to do?" cried Marv. "Steal my fans?"

**OPENING AT THE MET**

After the futile *Mets* had one of their rare good days, sweeping a twin bill from the *Braves*, a reporter chortled:

"You can't afford to give the *Mets* an opening. Make four or five mistakes against them and they can kill you."

**CASEY'S BEST BUDDY**

Casey had a first baseman in Brooklyn named Buddy

Hassett, who could tear your heart out with his Irish tenor. One winter the *Dodgers* set out for their Florida training camp by train. In the car with them was a baby who cried steadily from Newark to Baltimore.

Casey finally exploded. Taking Hassett by the arm, he walked over to the mother and child. "Madam," he said, "I'm the manager of the Brooklyn *Dodgers* and this is my left-handed tenor singer, Buddy Hassett. He'll now sing your infant to sleep."

The left-handed tenor began to croon, "Mighty Lak a Rose"—and the baby went right to sleep, and stayed that way until well beyond Richmond.

Casey returned to his seat. Nudging a columnist next to him, he said, "I have my critics, but they can't say I don't get the most out of my players."

**HE KNOWS THE SCORE**

Watching Herb Score's stiff movements in spring practice, Casey shook his head and said:

"Wild man Rex Barney was like that just before he washed out. His arm still had the power to throw the ball through a wall, but you couldn't be quite sure which building."

**SEE HOW THEY RUN**

The *Cubs* presented their starter, Bob Anderson, with a four-run lead in the first inning. Then the *Mets* came up. There followed in order a bunt single, a sacrifice, a walk, a sharp single, and a long triple. But the fellow who tripled, Marv Throneberry (who else?), got himself called out for failing to touch first base. The next batter then hit a homer, tying the score, 4–4, but not, of course, bringing in the run that Throne-berry would have represented.

"Anderson has given up four runs," the official scorer announced, "five of them earned."

**WALKS IN THE SUN**

Desperate for pitching help, Casey Stengel reached down to Class D for a 19-year-old with a good fast ball, no control, and a colossal conceit. The day after the rookie arrived, Stengel started him against the *Phillies*. The youth promptly walked the first five men to face him, getting over only two strikes. The *Mets'* manager sadly plodded out to the mound and waved to the bullpen.

The rookie came storming into the dugout, and slammed his glove down on the bench. "How do you like that big jerk?" he snarled.

"Look, kid," gently remonstrated one of the veterans, "the Old Man had to yank you. After all, you walked five men in a row."

"Yeah, but I had a no-hitter going!" snapped the rookie.

**BOOTING ONE**

A New York restaurant features a "Mets Room" with pictures of the ballplayers plastered all over the walls. During the football season a fellow came in with a photo of Don Chandler, the great kicker of the football *Giants*. He asked the restaurant manager to hang it on the wall.

"Sorry," he was told, "the room is reserved for the *Mets*."

"You're making a mistake," the fellow said. "You got

so many guys who kick the ball that you ought to show one who gets paid for doing it."

**IT RALLY HAPPENS**

It's now a tradition to regard any *Yankee* defeat as "good for baseball." Among the writers covering the *Mets*, it's customary to announce " . . . another bad day for baseball" whenever the scoreboard shows a *Yankee* victory.

Late in the 1962 season a writer looked up just in time to see the scoreboard put up four runs for the *Yankee* opponents. "Hey, look at the *Yankee* game," he called out. "Baseball has just rallied for four runs."

**TO THEM WHO SIT**

After getting his first look at all the culls and cast-offs on the New York *Mets*, Warren Spahn shook his head and murmured:

"I can see it now: Opening Day, and they've just finished playing the national anthem. Casey Stengel shouts to his players, 'Go get 'em!' But only Gil Hodges and Charlie Neal run onto the field. The rest of them are so used to sitting on the bench they just keep on sitting."

**SERPENTINE LOGIC**

Manager Stengel of the *Mets* has always been plagued by weak catchers, particularly lacking one who can handle low pitches.

"What we need behind the bat," he says, "is a snake with a mitt."

**STOCK**
**IN THE METS' CHANCES**

In a desire to help his beloved but dreadful *Mets*, a fan cornered Barney Kremenko, a local sportswriter.

"The *Yankees* get such great publicity mileage out of M & M for 'Mantle-and Maris'," he suggested, "why don't you start writing about our T & T for 'Thomas-and-Throneberry'?"

"That's not bad," admitted Barney. "But I'll tell you what: I'll add 'Ashburn' to make it A T & T—and that hasn't been doing so well either."

**A GENIUS**
**FOR WINNING**

Two-second interview with Casey Stengel:

"They say I'm a genius and Mr. George Weiss is a genius. But it don't do you no good if the ballplayers ain't geniuses, too."

**UPPER BERTHS**

Asked why the *Mets* didn't give away many autographed balls last season, Casey Stengel apologetically explained:

"We couldn't. Too many of our baseballs disappeared into the upper stands."

**DRY RUN**

Being interviewed at the *Mets'* training camp, Roger Craig shook his head sadly. "I can't pitch out here," he complained. "My spitter dries up halfway to the plate."

**LONG DISTANCE**

Pitching against Ernie Banks, Roger Craig kept shaking off the catcher. Finally the backstop walked out and muttered:

"You're gonna have to throw him something. Why don't you pitch?"

"Let's wait a while," Craig replied. "Maybe he'll get a long-distance call."

**EARLY WORMS**

Cookie Lavagetto, the *Mets'* coach, was always bugged by the early-season saw that the hitters are ahead of the pitchers. Last spring he disgustedly watched the *Mets* boot ball after ball.

Turning to a reporter, he sighed, "I see the grounders are ahead of the fielders."

**UPS AND DOWNS**

The ump wasn't very experienced. When the runner came into the bag in a cloud of dust, he called him safe. Then, seeing that the runner had overslid the bag, he made a quick change, putting his right hand up but keeping his left down in the original "safe" sign.

The runner looked up in bewilderment. "Mister," he asked, "which hand means what it says?"

**LEADERSHIP—
METS' STYLE**

A good ball team has a leader, a player it can look up to, a take-charge guy who can fire 'em up when they're dragging.

Norm Sherry, the catcher for the *Mets*, explained how it was in 1962.

"Duke Snider was our leader. The guys really looked up to him. We were like a football team. Duke would fire us up and we'd rush out, tearing the door off its hinges. Then we'd lose."

**ENGLISH ON THE BALL**

The Alou brothers, Felipe and Matty, are the best-hitting brother act since the great Waner brothers. Felipe, being older, has been around a bit and is at ease with the press. Matty, just a rookie in 1961, is painfully shy. Vin Scully, the voice of the *Dodgers*, asked Felipe about Matty.

"Doesn't he speak much English?"

"No," said Felipe, "and not much Spanish either."

**LOW BLOW**

Wild-swinging Bill Skowron swung at a low pitch. The ball got away from the catcher, advancing a base-runner. The official scorekeeper was torn between calling it a passed ball and a wild pitch.

"If it hit the dirt in front of the plate, naturally it's a wild pitch," he said, thinking aloud. "But I'm not absolutely sure whether it hit the dirt."

"Of course it hit the dirt," a reporter wisecracked. "Skowron swung at it, didn't he?"

**RUNNING BATTLE**

The dreadful old *White Sox* were getting massacred in Boston. Poor Mike Kreevich, the center fielder, ran until his tongue was hanging out. Finally he got to the bench, sank down, and groaned:

"I'm done. I can't run anymore."

The *Sox* quickly made out, and poor Mike had to go out there again. As he picked up his glove, he turned to his teammate, Bob Kennedy, and said:

"The worst of it is that when I'm pickin' up the balls near the stands, I keep seein' that sign: DOUBLEHEADER TOMORROW—AND SUNDAY."

### CAUGHT IN THE DRAFT

It was pointed out to Gene Mauch, *Phillies'* manager, that until the *Yankees* drafted Bill Kunkel for 1963, Gene had been the only other *Yankee* draft choice in over eighteen years.

"That's why the *Yankees* are so great," grinned Mauch. "They make a mistake only once every ten years."

### PRESIDENTIAL STRAIN

Before the 1962 All-Star Game in Washington, General Pete Quesada took personal charge of the opening-ball throwing ceremony involving the late President Kennedy. He instructed Earl Battey, American League starting catcher:

"Stand close to the stands because we don't want the President to strain his arm."

"What's the matter?" Battey wanted to know. "Did he pitch a doubleheader yesterday?"

### ASLEEP AT THE SWITCH

Dan Daniel, dean of baseball writers, is always doing the interview type of story. Nearly everything he writes is enclosed with quotation marks, much to the amusement of his fellow writers.

One afternoon a young reporter, entering the Yankee Stadium press box, noticed Daniel fast asleep over his typewriter. He reached over to wake him, only to be stopped by an older writer.

"Leave Dan alone, son," drawled the veteran, "he's interviewing Abner Doubleday."

**IN THE STRETCH**

During the spring training season, the *Reds* take strenuous calisthenics before every game. Before a *Reds–Yankee* game one April, Ralph Houk watched the *Reds* huffing and puffing through their push-ups and sit-ups. He then yelled to the *Reds'* manager, Fred Hutchinson:

"Hey, Hutch, what time's the kickoff?"

**STANDING CALL**

The new *Senators* and the old (now the *Twins*) happened to arrive at the Washington airport at the same time. Watching the players milling around, waiting for their baggage, a reporter cracked:

"Will the real Washington *Senators* please stand."

**JET LAUNCHING**

En route to Los Angeles shortly after Joe Gordon was fired in Kansas City and Cookie Lavagetto was bounced by Minnesota, *Yankee* manager Ralph Houk quipped:

"Can a manager be fired while traveling to a game in a jet?"

Coach Frank Crosetti comforted him:

"Don't worry, Skipper, if they fire you en route they give you a parachute before they tell you to jump."

**TALL STORY**

The Philadelphia *Eagles* spent a weekend at the same hotel as the Washington *Senators*. The lobby was loaded with football and baseball players, but nobody had any trouble telling which was which. As Danny O'Connell, the infielder put it:

"It's easy to pick out the football players. Every one of them looks like Harmon Killibrew's big brother."

**SALES PITCH**

Shopping in a Kansas City department store, hurlers Tom Sturdivant and Dick Donovan got separated. Sturdivant finally tracked Donovan down.

"Dick," he said excitedly, "I just saw Harry Truman in the hat department!"

"Buying or selling?" drawled Donovan.

**MOB SCENE**

Some years ago Bill Phelon, a Cincinnati sportswriter, began his story with:

"Before a large and enthusiastic crowd today the Cincinnati *Reds* . . ."

Next day his editor cornered him.

"What do you mean the crowd was large and enthusiastic? The AP says it was the smallest and quietest crowd of the season."

Phelon hung right in there.

"Well," he said, "Jackie Gleason was there. He's large; I'm enthusiastic."

**MONEY COUNTER**

Pistol Pete Reiser, *Dodger* coach, enjoys telling of the time he was managing Green Bay in a game against Cedar Rapids:

"My man, Frank Howard, who got a $108,000 bonus, lifted a dinky fly back of shortstop. Dennis Menke, their $115,000 shortstop; Bob Click, their $75,000 center fielder; and Bob Taylor, their $100,000 left fielder, went for the ball. But I can't remember who caught it. I was too busy counting their money."

**A FINE CASE**

When Rogers Hornsby was managing Beaumont, his catcher was Elvin Tappe. One night Elvin was beaned by the pitcher and ordered back to the hotel. It just happened that his twin brother, Mel, had attended the game, and later that night decided to see how Elvin was feeling.

As Mel walked through the lobby some time after midnight, Hornsby's stern voice arrested him.

"That will cost you $25 for breaking curfew, Elvin."

Mel continued to Elvin's room, where his brother assured him he was okay.

"That's good," replied Mel, "because Hornsby just fined you $25 for coming in late."

**WHEN TIMES WERE GRIMM**

A skinny kid approached Charlie Grimm while he was conducting a try-out camp during the war.

"I'm 4F," said the kid, "and I can hit like Stan Musial, throw harder than Bob Feller, and play the field better than Joe DiMaggio. And if you need me I can coach, too."

"You're nuts," was the Grimm retort.

"Sure," said the kid, "that's why I'm 4F."

**DRINK TO ME ONLY . . .**

Gene Hermanski and Chuck Connors (now "The Rifleman") came up to the *Dodgers* together. They met in the anteroom of the *Dodger* front office, and Hermanski went in to see Branch Rickey first. After an hour or so, he came out and Connors asked him how it went.

"Everything was going along all right," said Gene, "until he asked me if I drank. I said a little now and then, and he hit the ceiling."

Forewarned, Connors went in to see the Holy Man, who fired the same questions at him.

"Do you smoke?"

"No, Mr. Rickey."

"Do you go out with women?"

"No, Mr. Rickey."

"Do you drink?"

Connors brought his fist down on the desk and shouted, "If I have to drink to stay in your organization I'm leaving!"

**WHO, WHEN, WHAT, AND WIRE**

After receiving an unsigned contract, Hank Greenberg immediately sent a wire to the player:

IN YOUR HASTE TO ACCEPT THE TERMS
YOU FORGOT TO SIGN THE CONTRACT

The player came back with this note:

IN YOUR HASTE TO GIVE ME A RAISE,
YOU PUT IN THE WRONG FIGURE

**EXTRA PAIGE**

The ageless Satch Paige was called on for a ninth-inning relief stint in Washington. Bill Veeck, the *Browns'* boss, told the pitcher that the team had to catch a train in less than an hour. Paige struck out the side on only ten pitches.

"Sorry about that extra pitch," he apologized to Veeck as they boarded the train. "But the umpire missed one."

**OVER THE COUNTER**

After Satch helped the Indians win the 1948 American League flag, he was approached by a reporter.

"Think you'll pitch in the Series, Satch?"

"Nope, ain't likely."

"Why not?"

"Counter," replied Satch.

"What do you mean, 'counter'?" asked the puzzled writer.

"Counter Feller, Lemon, Beardon, and Gromek," was Paige's reply.

**ANOTHER PAIGE**

Rogers Hornsby met Satch Paige for the first time in the spring of 1952, when he took over as manager of the St. Louis *Browns.*

"We're a couple of old-timers," Hornsby told Satch, "and we've got to show these kids how to train. We old-timers have to set an example by working hard."

"Only trouble is," answered Paige, "that one of us old-timers gotta pitch."

**SATCH-URATION POINT**

Satch would think nothing of showing up a half hour late for practice. One dark and gloomy afternoon he didn't show up at all. His manager, Lou Boudreau, cornered him in the dressing room next day.

"Why didn't you show up yesterday?" he demanded.

"They told me the game would be called off," drawled Paige.

"It wasn't called off until game time," snapped Lou. "And who's the *they* who told you that was going to happen?"

"Mah feet," replied Paige.

**FILM-FLAM**

At a big sports banquet, the pictures of thirty all-time greats were flashed on the screen. As luck would have it, one of the slides got reversed, showing Ted Williams as a right-handed hitter. This brought a sigh from Lefty Gomez.

"After ten years," he said, "I now find out why I was pitching wrong to Williams."

**A BOAST IN THE NOSE**

As a kid pitcher in the minor leagues, Lefty once found himself several months behind in his rent. One evening his landlady pressed him for her due.

Gomez tried to appeal to her. "Just think," he said, "some day you'll be able to say Lefty Gomez once lived here."

"Yes," she snapped, "and unless I see some money right now, I'll be able to say it tomorrow."

**UNDER THE BRIDGES**

Rocky Bridges, the wandering shortstop who's now a minor league manager, is one of the most nimble-tongued wits in the big leagues. Riding to a game some years ago, he spotted an old schoolhouse with all the windows broken out.

"Someone must have flunked chemistry," he noted.

**HIGHLY CHARGED CARDS**

Rocky figures he was the most expensive player in baseball in 1961. The *Cardinals* bought him then for $40,000.

"I played only four innings for them," he explains, "so I cost them $10,000 an inning."

**TILT THE SOIL**

With the *Angels*, Rocky roomed with Albie Pearson, who was even smaller than Rocky. Across the way, 250-pound Steve Bilko roomed with 245-pound Ted Kluszewski. Rocky wanted the club secretary to change the pairings.

"If you don't," he warned, "the hotel will tilt."

**ON THE DOWNGRADE**

It was Rocky who remarked of 5-6 Albie Pearson, "It's restful warming up with Albie before a game. You're throwing downhill."

**SYMPTOM SIMON**

Back in 1920 a young pitcher named Huck Betts had a tryout with the *Phillies*. In his first game against Boston, he laid one down the pipe to Tony Boeckle, who drove it right back at him. The ball hit Betts squarely in the middle of the forehead, and he went out like a light. His manager, Wild Bill Donovan, rushed out and leaned over him.

"Are you all right? Are you all right?" he kept stuttering.

Betts opened his eyes and murmured drowsily, "No, Skipper, I haven't got a thing."

**MAID TO ORDER**

The Kansas City *Athletics*, having several knuckleball pitchers on the staff, keep a supply of those oversized catcher's mitts. Mel McGaha, a coach, keeps one in his room. One day the maid saw it and asked McGaha what it was.

"Oh, we use that to catch knuckleballs," explained Mel.

"Gee, are knuckleballs that big?" the maid asked.

**SHOCK THEATRE**

Sandy Koufax, who throws a block party every time he hits as much as a foul ball, astonished everyone, including himself, by whacking a bases-loaded homer during the 1963 season.

Back in the dressing room after the game, Sandy shook his head.

"You know, when I got to second base, I didn't know whether to continue or to stop and apologize to the pitcher."

**MUSIAL FOR READING**

When Stan Musial slumped to .255 in 1959, one of the St. Louis columnists wrote:

"Take my word for it, Stan Musial won't last another year."

When Stan hit .275 the next season, the same columnist wrote:

"I'm willing to bet that Musial won't be around in 1961."

When The Man bounced back with .330 in 1962, the columnist put in his final word:

"On this I'll stake my life: Musial won't last forever."

**SHOO, FLY,
DON'T BOTHER ME**

When Dave Nicholson came up to the *Orioles,* he exhibited lots of potential as a slugger but simply couldn't strike up an acquaintance with fly balls. Toward the end of the season, some of the writers thought he improved a bit.

"To be sure," Gordon Cobbledick wrote, "Nicholson hasn't caught a ball as yet, but he appears to be getting a little closer."

**THE NUMBERS RACKET**

Red Schoendienst wore the familiar No. 2 in his *Cardinal* comeback, borrowing it from Hal Smith, the catcher. Smitty was happy to oblige Red. As he explained it:

"When Red was with the *Cardinals* the first time, he wore No. 2 and had two children. When he was with the *Braves,* he wore No. 4 and had four children. When he returned to the *Cards* in 1961, they gave him No. 16. What else *could* I do?"

**LONG-RANGE BOMBING**

Mickey Mantle came into the 1961 World Series weak, beat, and crippled from surgery. But he gave it a game try.

During his first batting practice turn in Cincinnati, he staged one of the most breathtaking performances in Series history. Batting righty against practice-pitcher Spud Murphy, Mantle clouted the first four serves over the left-field fence, the fifth against the fence, and the sixth and seventh pitches against the scoreboard.

Mickey made no effort to conceal his exuberance:

"Come on, Spud," he shouted gleefully, "give me a good ball to hit!"

**TAKES IT FROM THE TOP**

During spring training, Clem Labine, the *Mets'* relief pitcher, went in for a lot of yogi exercises. One day Roger Craig strolled by and discovered Clem standing on his head. He watched him for a while, then drawled,

"What are you doing, Clem? Going over the hitters?"

**FREEZE ENTERPRISE**

From *Baseball Digest:*

"Baseball is a game in which the young man who bravely strikes out for himself receives no praise for his enterprise."

**ASSAULT AND BUTTERY**

When that essence of sweetness, Billy Martin, slugged the young *Cub* pitcher, Johnny Brewer, fracturing his cheek, he was fined $500 by the league prexy. Martin's teammates, sympathetic for some strange reason, chipped in to defray the fine.

A week later Martin was sued by the *Cubs* for $1,040,000.

His teammates, still sympathetic but now amused, assured Martin of their support.

Martin's initial reaction to the suit was classic:

"I wonder if they want me to pay it in cash or by check."

"Don't worry, Billy," murmured a pal, "it'll cost us only $35,000 apiece."

**THE CURFEW**
**SHALL NOT RING TONIGHT**

Upon being told to report immediately to the *Phillies*, the minor league player rushed from the airport to the *Philly* hotel in St. Louis. He went straight up to Manager Gene Mauch's room and rapped on the door. A sleepy-eyed, pajama-clad manager opened the door.

"What do you want?" he rasped.

"I was told to report to you *immediately*," the rookie replied. "So here I am."

Mauch looked at his watch. It was 4 A.M. "Hell," he thought, "I'll teach this kid a lesson." So he told the rookie to go around to each player's room and introduce himself.

The kid returned at 4:30 A.M.

"Well," asked Mauch, repressing a grin, "what did the players say?"

"Nothing," said the rookie. "None of them are in yet."

**HOT-HEIR CONDITIONING**

The veteran infielder was kidding the rookie pitcher,

"I hear you didn't do so well on your date with the owner's daughter last night."

"Terrible," groaned the rookie, "no hits, no runs, no heiress."

**SPREAD FORMATION**

Frank Sullivan, the big right-hander who once proudly announced that "I'm in the twilight of a mediocre career," was with the *Phillies* when they returned home after losing twenty-three in a row. Upon arriving at the airport, the players were amazed to find a group of fans waiting to greet them.

Sullivan quickly reached for the mike:

"Attention, all members of the *Phillies*," he announced. "Please walk at least fifty feet apart when leaving the plane. That way they won't get all of us with one burst."

**DRESSEN DOWN**

When managing the *Dodgers*, Charley Dressen used to scold Gil Hodges for never arguing with the umpires.

"Get on that ump when he calls that outside strike," Charley once told him, "and I'll give you $50."

Gil, always the class ballplayer, looked at Dressen coldly.

"Charley," he answered, "I've got $50."

**A RUSSIAN LULLABY**

During his brief stay with the *Cubs*, the fabulous Mad Russian, Lou Novikoff, proved he could do it with the bat but that he was strictly from butcherville with the glove.

One afternoon the *Cubs* went into the bottom of the

ninth leading by a run. The opponents got two men on base and, with two out, the hitter lined toward Novikoff. The Mad Russian came tearing in, stubbed his toe, and fell flat on his face. The ball went all the way to the fence, the runners scored, and the *Cubs* had lost again.

As the players trudged to the clubhouse, the manager approached his errant outfielder.

"What happened, Lou?" he asked.

Novikoff blinked. "Where?"

**PASSION IN THE RAIN**

Lindsey Nelson, NBC's top telecaster, and his partner, Fred Haney, ex-manager of the *Braves*, toured Germany entertaining our troops. During their stop-over in Oberammergau, they went through the unique auditorium that houses the famed *Passion Play*. The guide explained that the section for the audience is roofed, but the stage has only the sky for its ceiling—and that even if it rains during a performance, the show must go on.

"They have two sets of costumes," the guide told them, "in the event they get too wet."

"How long does a performance last?" asked Haney.

"About seven and a half hours," said the guide.

"No wonder they have to play in the rain," said Haney. "They can't play two tomorrow."

**TWO FOR THE MONEY**

"How many players would it take to make Kansas City a pennant winner?" Ed Lopat was asked.

"Just two," replied the A's manager.

"Only two? You're kidding."

"No, sir," smiled Lopat. "Just Walter Johnson and Babe Ruth."

### . . . IS WORTH TWO IN THE BUSHES

When Clarence Rowland was making his managerial debut with the *White Sox*, he vehemently protested a close play at second. Umpire Dick Nallin, then also a rookie, finally lost his patience.

"You're through, busher," he shouted. "I've seen enough of you for today."

"Just what I was afraid of," sadly replied Rowland. "I knew that I'd get the gate sooner or later, but I expected some real big leaguer to chase me. I thought us bushers would be sticking together."

### SEVEN-LEAGUE BOOTS

The prince of sports humorists, John Lardner, once wrote that Boots Poffenberger, a right-handed pitcher for the Dodgers, had a lot of stuff. "He drank a lot of stuff," said one of his teammates, "so why shouldn't he have it?"

"The curfew was midnight for the *Dodgers*," wrote John, "and Poffenberger was almost always in by midnight—by San Francisco time when the team was in Cincinnati, by Honolulu time when the team was in St. Louis."

### TIME FOR DECISION

Jocko Conlon, the veteran balls-and-strikes arbiter, offers this brief apologia for his beleaguered profession:

"We have two seconds to render a decision. The Supreme Court has two years."

**PERMANENT SITTER**

After Puddinhead Jones, the ancient third baseman, was dealt to the *Reds*, he sank into embarrassing obscurity.

"I've been sitting on the bench so long," sighed Willie some time later, "that the kids are beginning to call me 'Judge.' "

**A CLOSE SHAVE**

Before being dumped unceremoniously by Kansas City, Manager Joe Gordon won a big game and decided to treat his coaches to a meal. The happy masterminds met at the appointed hour, except for Coach Jo-Jo White. Gordon called him up.

"Sorry, Joe," said Jo-Jo, "I'm not ready yet. Suppose I join you later."

"What's holding you up?" asked Gordon.

"Well, I still gotta shave."

"Okay, we'll see you later then. You can rush it by using my Norelco."

"Thanks, Joe, but it isn't really necessary. I'll grab a cab."

**A WHIFF AND AN ERROR**

Bob Bauman, the former trainer of the *Giants*, was a great practical joker. One day, after a hard workout, Johnny Mize came into the clubhouse drenched with perspiration. He took off his sweatshirt and went to get a drink of water. Bauman promptly soaked the sweatshirt with alcohol. When Mize returned, Bauman asked him how he felt.

"Tired, but good."

"Better stay away from that hard stuff, though, John. That's what really gets you," Bauman kindly said.

"What do you mean, 'hard stuff'? I only had a couple of beers and was in early last night."

"Oh yeah?" replied Bauman. "Don't kid me. Look."

He dropped a match on the sweatshirt and it went up in flames. "That's alcohol you sweated out, John!"

Mize grabbed for the shirt. "Doc, Doc," he pleaded, "don't say anything about this to anyone."

**STUNTED CURVE**

When Grover Powell pitched in the Florida Instructional League in 1962, he couldn't get his curveball up to the plate. The hooks kept bouncing off the chest and shoulders of Choo Choo Coleman.

"That man," muttered Choo Choo, "has the best 55-foot curve I've ever seen."

**CHANNEL NO. 5**

At one time Grover considered himself something of a cartoonist.

"I specialized in kook characters," explained the young *Mets'* pitcher, "and I thought I was doing pretty well. I finally sent my work to a famous cartoonist and asked him if there was some channel for my talent. He told me yes—the English Channel."

**HECKLE AND HIDE**

Glenn Ewing, baseball coach at Helena, Oklahoma,

was taking a steady heckling from a fan during a ball game. Ewing kept ignoring the taunts, being preoccupied with the opposing pitcher's motion toward first base. The boy was continually using a snap throw in his attempts to pick off the baserunners.

Ewing finally called the umpire's attention to the rule stipulating that a pitcher must ". . . step with the non-pivot foot toward a base while throwing." The ump consulted his rule book, ruled a balk, and sent the Helena runner to second base.

Ewing returned to the bench, a trifle smugly, to be greeted by the voice of his heckler:

"Okay, buddy, after arguing for twenty years you were bound to be right sometime."

**PIGSKIN PENALTY**

A baseball team was practicing on a large field, and the shortstop hit the ball a long way into center field. Before the fielder could get to the drive, a pig ran out and swallowed the ball. Everyone started arguing about the ruling on the play. The umpire finally ruled that it was an *inside-the-pork* home run.

**COUP DE GRACE— SMITH STYLE**

Columnist Red Smith is a small, gentle, civilized fellow who rarely gets his dander up. One of the few people who ever brought out the beast in him was Happy Ah Love Baseball Chandler. Red thought he was a mountebank, and when

Happy finally got the can tied to his tail Red swiftly administered the coup de grace:

"Nothing that Happy Chandler did in his six unquiet years as baseball commissioner becomes him as well as his leave-taking. Not many men can achieve an air of perfect nonchalance when they have been publicly divested of their pants."

## BUNTING CIRCA 1985

According to old-timers who insist that the jack-rabbit baseball and home runs have "ruined" the national pastime, the following scene (as created by the gifted New York sportswriter, Leonard Koppett) could take place in any big league dugout today.

MANAGER: All right, kid, I want you to go up there and bunt.

PLAYER: You want me to do what?

MANAGER: Bunt.

PLAYER: Punt? That's football—you know, on fourth down.

MANAGER: Not punt—BUNT with a B.

PLAYER: Where am I going to catch a bee?

MANAGER: Look, I'm talking about a sacrifice bunt. You hold the bat this way, see? With the hands apart . . .

PLAYER: Hands apart? Are you kidding, grandpa? Who holds a bat with the hands apart? They showed me back in the Little League to grip it down here on the handle and . . .

MANAGER: I'm telling you, hands apart. Now you square around and face the pitcher like this . . .

PLAYER: Face the pitcher? Are you nuts? My high school coach told me . . .

# Shakespeare on Baseball

Illustrated by Charles Beck

"Where go you with bats and clubs?"
(Coriolanus)

"Thou canst not hit it, hit it, hit it; thou canst not hit, my good man."
(Love's Labor Lost)

"Let me be umpire in his doubtful strife."
(Henry IV)

"And so I shall catch the fly."
(Henry V)

"Primo, secundo, tertio is a good play."
(Twelfth Night)

MANAGER: Will you shut up and listen? I want you to hold the bat like this and just tap the ball in front of the plate.

PLAYER: Hey, you guys, listen to this—the skipper has flipped his lid. He wants me to just tap the ball in front of the plate—on purpose—what in the world for?

MANAGER [*patiently*]: It's called a sacrifice bunt. While they run in to field it and throw you out, our runner on first can get to second.

PLAYER: You want me to make out on purpose? They gave me a $150,000 bonus to make out on purpose?

MANAGER: You don't understand . . .

PLAYER [*more indignant*]: A guy asked me to do something like that when I was on the freshman basketball team in college and I reported it to my coach. I think I'll report you to the Commissioner right now.

MANAGER [*a little desperate*]: Look, it's not what you think at all. Anyway, this is just an inter-squad game. Let me show you what I mean. I'll go up and do it myself. You just watch. [*The manager goes to the plate. The pitcher pitches. The manager bunts. The ball sails over the right field fence. The manager stares, stupefied.*]

PLAYER [*disapprovingly, to teammates*]: He'll never get anywhere with that stance. How can he pull an outside pitch?

**LET THE PUNISHMENT FIT THE CRIME**

Seems there was this $75,000 bonus pitcher who was farmed out to an A club. Nervous as a kitten, he walked ten men in the first inning of his initial start, repeated this performance several times, and soon had amassed an 0–5 record.

The kid's roomie buttonholed the manager:

"Look, skipper," he said, "why do you tell him he's going to pitch? He gets so nervous, he can't sleep all night. He keeps pacing the floor and vomiting. I suggest that you don't tell him when he's going to start. Give him the ball five minutes before the game, and see what happens."

So the manager decided to try this new approach. Sure enough, the kid proceeded to win fifteen in a row, including seven shut-outs. Then came the playoffs. The team loses the first; the rookie gets the surprise starting assignment, and wins. Later he wins again. Finally it's 3–3. The kid guesses he's going to throw the final one. He gets the assignment all right and, nervous as a cat, he gets trounced 15–0.

The manager stalks into the clubhouse and promptly starts berating every man on the club, in each case finishing with, "And I hope I never see you again!" The rookie pitcher is cowering in the corner. He has been saved for last. All eyes are turned on him as the manager strolls over. But, to everyone's amazement, the manager adopts a completely different manner. He puts his arm around the kid's shoulders and coos:

"Now, young feller, I want you to know that I'm completely satisfied with you. You did a great job." He pats the kid on the head and turns away. The kid is beaming. The manager then turns his head back and in the same soft voice, adds:

"Oh, by the way. I want you to know that you're going to be my starting pitcher in the opener next spring. Now go home and I hope you *don't sleep the whole damned winter!*"

& &

&

# VI. Mostly Horse Laughs

### OFF FORMERLY

*In a recent tennis match between Vic Seixas and Dick Savitt, a couple of hoary amateurs, the announcer introduced Seixas as "... formerly winner at Wimbledon, formerly Australian champion, formerly U.S. champion, ..." Then he introduced Savitt as "... formerly Australian champion, formerly U.S. National champion, ..."*

*At which point a paying customer caustically shouted, "Yeah, and formerly this would have been a helluva good match!"*

**STRING INSTRUMENT**

Covering his first tennis tournament, the visiting sportswriter was astounded to see a boy playing a match with a two-handed grip on a banjo.

"Good lord!" the scribe yelled to the umpire. "Why don't you tell him he's supposed to use a racket!"

"We can't now," the umpire calmly replied. "He's just reached the semi-finals."

**LOVE, SET, MATCH**

Ralph Kiner was telling his broadcasting buddy, Lindsey Nelson, about his wife, the former tennis star, Nancy Chaffee.

"When I married Nancy, I vowed I'd beat her at tennis some day. After six months, she beat me 6–2. After a year, she beat me 6–4. After we were married a year and a half, I pushed her to 7–5. Then it happened—she had a bad day and I had a good one, and I beat her 17–15."

"Good for you, Ralph," exclaimed Lindsey. "Did she have any alibi?"

"Of course not!" Kiner snapped indignantly. "She was only eight months pregnant."

**WHEN THE SUN SHINES**

Possibly the most charming and erudite fencing coach in captivity, Oscar F. Kolombatovich (sounds like one of those old Notre Dame tackles) is, among other things, Fencing Master of the Metropolitan Opera Company, Coach at West Point, Director of the Huntington (New York) Fencing Academy, Editor-in-Chief of the official publication of the National Fencing Coaches Association, a masterful designer and builder of fencing equipment, an anthropologist, and a distinguished historian.

Among the many other things we like about the gentleman is his rapier-like sense of humor. One day at his Academy he was trying to teach his son a complex fencing phrase, but the kid simply couldn't get it. Oscar, a versatile linguist, unloosed a long string of invective—in several different languages.

A little old lady, watching the lesson, went into shock.

"Mr. Kolombatovitch!" she scolded. "You shouldn't use language like that! God will hear you!"

Oscar turned his fine head in the woman's direction and neatly riposted,

"Madam, I think He'd understand. He had a Son, too."

**HALE FELLOWS, WELL MET**

At Kolombatovich's fencing classes at the Metropolitan

Opera House, the girls invariably show up in skin-tight leotards. One afternoon Louis Sgarro, the basso, exploded.

"Please, girls," he rumbled, "put on some clothes. Those leotards are too distracting. I can't concentrate on the fencing."

Ezio Flagello, a fellow basso, promptly bellowed back:

"*Animale!* Shut up! Do you think I come here to *fence?*"

**FISH STORY**

Ted Williams was prouder of his fishing exploits than all his great batting records.

"I may not be the greatest hitter who ever lived," he once bragged to Jack Fadden, the *Red Sox* trainer, "but no one can deny that I'm the greatest fisherman!"

"Oh, I don't know about that," said Fadden. "There was somebody who lived a long time ago who caught more fish in one scoop than you'll catch in your lifetime."

"And who," Williams asked belligerently, "the hell was that?"

"Our Lord," replied Fadden quietly.

Williams lapsed into silence—for one moment.

"Anyway," he said, "you had to go pretty far back to find somebody, didn't you?"

**CAUGHT OFF BASS**

Our favorite fisherman's tall tale concerns the angler who, disgruntled at his failure to catch anything, impulsively dipped the minnow he was using as bait into a jug of moonshine. Seconds later he hauled in a huge sea bass, which was threshing around helplessly against the minnow—who had it by the throat and was choking it to death.

**IMITATION HAM**

Softball is a favorite pastime of the casts of Broadway plays. One afternoon two teams of actors were playing a league game. At a critical moment in a late inning, the manager of one of the teams called for a pinch hitter. Off the bench came a fellow wearing jeans, sneakers, and an old T-shirt, just like Marlon Brando.

"Look," said a bystander watching the game, "they're sending in a pinch mumbler."

**THE SECRET SEVEN**

The late Tom O'Reilly had a wonderfully witty way with words. Though his consuming passion was horseflesh, every now and then he liked to commune with nature or other forms of wild life—like college crew. His bright, civilized good humor was beautifully exemplified in the lead paragraph of a rowing story he once wrote for *Sport:*

> **If I ever have to hide from the police (a thought which is constantly on my mind), I have the spot picked out. I will try to win a position on a college crew, preferably in the center of the boat.**

**LEADING WITH THE RITE**

O'Reilly had a miserable day at the track and was down to his last deuce when, just before the final race, he happily caught sight of his parish priest annointing one of the horses.

"With the holy father blessin' the craiture," he reasoned, "how kin he lose?"

He put his last two bucks on the horse—which finished a dead last.

Several days later he encountered the priest on the street and grumbled, "Ye let me down, Father. I bet on a horse because ye stopped to bless it, and begorra, it finishes last!"

The priest shook his head sadly.

"You should have more faith than that, my boy. I wasn't blessing that horse. I was giving him last rites."

### THE ONE THAT GOT AWAY

After owning a horse for eight years, a fellow finally entered him in a race. Having no record, the nag went off at 90 to 1. He got off like a jet and zoomed around the track to win by twelve lengths. Naturally the stewards were suspicious, and called in the owner.

"How come you never raced this horse before?" they demanded. "After all, you've had him for eight years."

"To tell the truth," the owner sheepishly replied, "we couldn't catch him until he was seven."

### MUTUEL AFFECTION

One of the *Dodger* wives, much in need of a day off from her household chores, farmed out junior to hubby on an open date in the schedule. That evening, when junior and daddy returned, she asked what kind of time they had had.

"Just great, Mommy," enthused junior. "We went to the zoo—and one of the animals won and paid $22.80!"

**MILK-SOP**

As the horses prepared to go to the starting gate for the featured race, the millionaire owner addressed his oat burner—who hadn't won a race all season.

"I've spent money on you. You've lived well, traveled, eaten the best hay and oats. Yet you've never won a race. Win this one or, I swear, tomorrow morning you're pulling a milk wagon."

The horse started poorly and got worse. The jockey was whipping harder and harder. Finally the horse turned to the jockey and said:

"Hey, take it easy, will you? I gotta be up at four o'clock tomorrow morning!"

**NEIGH-BORLY THING TO DO**

As some of you probably know, it's the custom in Florida to give the profits of the first three days of all horse and dog track meetings to the state colleges to help defray athletic scholarships. This amounts to more than $250,000 a year.

Upon learning of this arrangement, John McGraw, the great old baseball manager, suggested that by way of repayment all horses and dogs should be admitted free to the football games at these colleges.

**SADDLE SAW**

The two (dumb)belles decided to take up horseback riding. Asked by the riding master as to their preferences in saddles, they looked blank. "What kind are available?" they wanted to know.

"There's the English saddle and the Western saddle," they were informed.

"What's the difference?"

"The English saddle is flat, and the Western saddle has a horn on it," explained the riding master.

"We'll take the English saddles," promptly replied the ladies. "We don't intend to ride in any traffic."

### IN AT THE FINISH

A bookie was testifying before a committee investigating honesty in horse racing.

"The boss gave me $25,000 to fix the race," he said. "There were four other horses in it, and I gave each jockey $5,000."

"That's only $20,000," interjected an investigator.

"I know," replied the bookie. "I needed the other $5,000 for the photographer in charge of finishes."

### MAKING HAY WHILE THE SUN SHINES

The mare had won the big race and was boasting about it to the colt in the adjoining stall.

"And besides," added the winner happily, "I was promised two extra bales of hay if I won the race. And, brother, that ain't money."

### HORSE CENSOR

Two race track addicts met on the way home from

Belmont, and one immediately began bemoaning his miserable luck. The other said:

"Why don't you try my system? Every morning I go to church and pray for fifteen minutes. Since I started, not a day has gone by that I haven't picked at least two winners."

"What have I got to lose?" muttered the unlucky one. "I'll try your system."

Three weeks later they met again, and the steady loser was still moaning.

"You and your advice," he snarled. "Not only did I pray every morning, but every evening as well. All day Sunday I spent in church, too, not to mention a couple of holidays. And in all that time I didn't have a single winner."

"I can't understand it," said his friend. "What church did you pray in?"

"The one on Merrill Street," was the answer.

"No wonder, you dope!" shouted the friend. "That's for trotters!"

**QUITTING TIME**

At the People-to-People sports salute to Mrs. Joan Payson, Joe E. Lewis, the famous comedian, asked Eddie Arcaro why he retired from the track.

"Well, Joe," replied Arcaro, "I wanted to quit when I was ahead."

"Oh ho," roared Joe E., "so that was my trouble. Every time I bet on you, you quit while you were ahead!"

& &

&

# VII. A Little Twit Of Everything

**P'S AND QUEUES**

The coach, though a slave-driver, was an emotional sort of man. One day, after dropping a boy from the squad, he put his arm around the boy's shoulders and throbbed, "You probably hate me for dropping you. You'll probably spit on my grave."

"Oh, no, Coach," the boy dryly retorted. I hate standing in line."

**BIG PRODUCTION**

When the youthful coach asked for a raise,

& &

&

the school's athletic director proved absolutely adamant.

"Son," he said, "you're already making as much as any other coach on the staff, and they all have families with two or three kids."

The young coach protested. "Look, I thought we got paid for what we produce on the field, not for what we produce at home on our own time."

**PLUG-GED**

The athletic director, checking on the references of a prospective assistant coach, called the applicant's former boss.

"How long did Tony work for you?" he inquired.

"Oh, about eight hours," was the answer.

"Eight hours!" exclaimed the A. D. "He told me he was with you for four years."

"He was, he was," answered the ex-boss.

**TEAM PROJECT**

It was a red-letter day for the coach, what with the announcement of his new book and his wife's new baby appearing simultaneously. He was heartily congratulated by his athletic director who added smilingly, "Of which are you prouder?"

The coach, thinking of the achievement which necessitated the greatest effort, modestly replied:

"Well, I couldn't have done it without the help of two graduate students."

**A BITING HECKLE**

The speaker had bored the sports banquet audience for almost an hour.

"After partaking of such a meal," he droned at one point, "I feel that if I had taken just one more bite I'd be unable to continue speaking."

From the end of the room a loud voice said, "Will someone please give that guy a sandwich."

**ON THE LEVEL**

Sign on Bill Snypp's desk in the Ohio State publicity office:

*If you can keep a level head in all this confusion, you just don't understand the problem.*

**TWIN-KILLING**

Coach Doaks of little Podunk U. entrained for the Midwest to be interviewed for a head coaching job at one of the big state universities. He took the porter aside.

"Look, buddy," he said, "I'm a terribly heavy sleeper. When we pull into University Park, make sure to wake me up. No matter how hard I resist, get me off the train."

When the coach awoke many hours later, the train was pulling out of St. Louis, 150 miles beyond his destination. Without a word, he grabbed the porter and started belting and kicking him. Still without a word, Doaks dropped the porter into a seat and left the car.

An interested observer went up to the porter and murmured sympathy. "Gee, but that man was rough on you."

"Yes, sir," replied the porter, "but not half as rough as the guy I put off at University Park."

**POSITIVELY THINKING**

The power of positive thinking by that time-honored mental marvel, *Anon.*:

> **You're either a successful coach or an unsuccessful one. If you're successful, you have nothing to worry about. If you're unsuccessful, you have only two things to worry about: you're either healthy or sick. If you're healthy, you don't have anything to worry about. If you're sick, you only have two things to worry about: you're going to recover or you're going to die. If you're going to recover, you don't have anything to worry about. If you're going to die, you have only two things to worry about: you're going to go to Heaven or you're going to that other place. If you're going to heaven, you don't have anything to worry about. If you're going to that other place, you're going to be so darned busy shaking hands with old coaching buddies that you won't have time to worry.**

**SWEET-SWAP**

Harold Weisman, the crack sports columnist, described the famous interchange of spies as follows:

"U-2 Pilot Francis Powers and a touring American student for Col. Rudolph Abel and a spy to be named later."

**REST AND EXERCISE**

In his address before the AAHPER convention, Attorney General Robert F. Kennedy commented on the physical fitness problem in this witty fashion:

"I am reminded of Bill Bingham's observation of a Saturday afternoon at Harvard's Memorial Stadium—22 boys on the field badly in need of rest, and 40,000 people in the stands badly in need of exercise."

**SLIPS THAT PASS IN THE NIGHT**

"Your honor," the woman complained in court, "my husband is an inveterate gambler. That's all he talks about—football games, baseball games, dice, and cards. He doesn't even remember the date on which we were married."

"That's a lie!" the husband yelled. "It was the day I crapped out in Nevada after seven straight passes!"

**A TURN-OUT FOR THE BETTER**

All his life, the coach had been a mean, selfish, arrogant, thoroughly detested individual. His teams were sullen, poorly coached, perennial losers. Nobody would go see them play. The university was about ready to release him, when the coach pulled a fast one. He crashed his car, and was instantly killed.

As a final tribute to the late unlamented mentor, the university put his body to lie in state in the middle of the stadium. The student body was given the day off to pay its final respects. They filled every one of the 25,000 seats.

A cynical sports columnist surveyed the huge assemblage, then murmured to the athletic director:

"See? I told you they'd turn out for something they liked."

**D-F AND DUMB**

The coach almost hemorrhaged when his star player produced his mid-term report card showing one D and six F's.

"Coach," the boy said unhappily, "what can I do to improve my grades?"

The coach pondered this one for a while.

"Son," he said at last, "it looks to me as though you're putting in too much time on one subject."

**OLYMPIAN PIQUE**

A couple of American women, taking in the wondrous sights of Rome in June of 1960, approached the Colosseum and gaped at the awesome splendor of this ancient landmark.

"Isn't it breathtaking," gasped one of the women.

"It's certainly impressive," admitted the other. "But it'll never be ready in time for the Olympics."

**PRAYER-IFIED ATMOSPHERE**

With team prayers becoming so fashionable these days, our coaches are putting a lot of pressure on the Lord. If every team prays so hard for victory, how is He going to accommodate everyone?

A reporter asked a priest just that question: "What would the Lord do if two teams prayed for victory with exactly the same fervor?"

The priest's eyes twinkled. "I imagine," he said, "that He would just sit back and enjoy a whale of a game."

**CRUELLEST CUT OF ALL**

After one of Uncle Sam's frustrating periods in the 1960 Olympics, a girl was overheard asking her boy friend, "What happened in the Olympics today?"

He retorted, "Nothing happens on Sunday."

She replied, "It's a good thing—we'd have finished second in church."

**FUNDAMENTALLY SPEAKING**

Golden nugget of advice to all sports banquet speakers:

The elements of a good speech are a good beginning, a good ending, and having them close together.

**THE LETTER-BUG**

The proud father was bragging about his son, a great all-around athlete but a complete dunce in the classroom.

"My boy won his fourth letter this winter," he boasted to his business partner.

"Very true," replied the other quietly, "but I bet you had to read it to him."

**ADVICE TO THE LOVELORN**

The team captain broke training by coming in four hours after curfew. Afraid to face his coach the next day, he wrote:

*Dear Coach: I'm sorry, but I stayed out very late last night with my girl. Did I do wrong?*

The coach wrote back:

*Try to remember.*

**UPON DOING THE IMPOSSIBLE**

Here's an inspirational message for athletes who are called upon to do the "impossible" by their coaches:

*The scoffers said it couldn't be done,*
*And the odds were so great, who wouldn't?*
*So I tackled the job that couldn't be done,*
*And what do you know? It couldn't!*

**IN OVER HIS HEAD**

The tyrannical, overweening athletic director called in the basketball coach and said, "I've heard you've been to church praying for a raise. Don't you know I won't stand for anyone going over my head?"

### A BANQUET FIT FOR A KINK

Red Smith on the subject of sports banquets:

In the millenium, no doubt, it will be a hanging offense for more than eight people to graze together, but anybody who thinks that will be a deterrent is living in a fool's paradise. The winter sports banquet will simply go underground, like the Christians in ancient Rome . . . .

Not only has mass feeding become a part of our culture; it is spreading like impetigo in a boys' camp. . . . No light of hope twinkles on the horizon of the future. The threat of the gibbet is not going to faze a nation that can sit with its belly full of overdone beef and stare back unafraid at a dais as formidable as a Castro firing squad.

This is the real reason baseball clubs spend large sums to segregate their help in hideouts like Clearwater, Fla., and Scottsdale, Ariz. It is not for exercise . . . but to find sanctuary from the vulcanized chicken, the peas fabricated by Remington Arms and Ammunition, the introductory greetings and the closing remarks.

### THE SOUND BARRIER

As the *Talmud* advises:

*Eating should be done in silence lest the windpipe open before the gullet, and life be in danger.*

And, if it's permissible to quote Phyllis McGinley:

*Whenever public speakers rise*
*To dazzle hearer and beholders,*
*A film comes over both my eyes.*
*Inevitably, toward my shoulders*
*I feel my head begin to sink.*
*It is an allergy, I think.*

**THE MARRA**
**THE MERRIER**

High school coaches usually take a back seat in the after-dinner speaking department, but not Frank (Chic) Marra. The Dickson City (Pennsylvania) High School mentor is a four-alarm fire at banquets. Here's a fair sampling of his wit and wisdom:

**If all the cigarettes were laid end to end, they'd encircle the earth. If all the basketball officials were laid end to end . . . you know, that's a good idea.**

**It's a known fact that women play an important part in a coach's life. There's a woman behind every successful man. Napoleon had his Josephine. Washington had his Martha. Eisenhower has his Mamie. Even Heinz has his . . . tomatoes.**

**It's a bad policy to have your children witness arguments between you and your wife. We have a policy in our home that whenever we have an argument, we send the children out to buy ice cream. Do you know we have two of the fattest kids on the block?**

**I never heard of the words "juvenile delinquent" when I was a kid. Maybe we were spoiled brats or maybe we didn't have any money. I came from a large family. We had ten children. Being the youngest, I**

**used to get all the hand-me-down clothing, and it was quite embarrassing. You see, I had nine sisters. Do you know I was twelve years old when the boys stopped carrying my books home?**

**But I was different from the other kids. Even when I was in kindergarten I was different from the other five-year-olds: I was twelve years old.**

**In my avocation as a humorist, I come into contact with all types of audiences. But the group that impressed me most was the veterans at the V.A. hospital in Wilkes-Barre. Making the disabled laugh is quite a challenge.**

**As I finished my stories and was leaving the ward one year, I waved at them and said, "So long, fellas, I hope you get better." One of the veterans braced himself in his wheelchair and waved right back. "So long, Chic, I hope you get better, too."**

### REPEAT PERFORMANCE

The local doctor, a prominent alumnus, was asked to give the boys a pep talk at a rally before the first game. Throughout his enthusiastic speech, he kept repeating, "Give 'em hell, boys! When you get in there, give 'em H-E-L-L."

The next speaker, a mild-mannered minister, then rose and in a small voice said, "Boys, give 'em what the doctor ordered."

### A NIGHT OF TERRIER

Covering a dog show, Red Smith raved about ". . . a Boston terrier in a crimson turtle-neck sweater who looked like the Harvard captain of '97."

**OWN WORST ENEMY**

When Gump Worsley was tending net for the pathetic *Rangers*, he was asked to name the team that gave him the most trouble.

"That's easy," he immediately replied, "the *Rangers*."

**BLOOD AND SAND(MAN)**

The local sports columnist was interviewing the most famous athlete in the community.

"One thing puzzles me," he said. "You're all-state in basketball, football, baseball, and track. You also compete on the swimming, wrestling, tennis, golf, and fencing teams. Man, when do you sleep?"

"That's easy," replied the star. "During practices."

**OOH, YOU NASH-TY MAN!**

The enormously witty Ogden Nash scored again in his hilarious collection of barking doggerel, *Everyone But Thee and Me*. Here's the way he delectably assassinated the calisthenic-mad brotherhood and sisterhood aboard ship in a poem entitled "A Day on a Cruise":

*A maelstrom of fun that will not end*
*Till maelstrom and femalestrom end,*

when—

*Comes a whoop like the Sioux in pursuit of the Senecas,*
*It's the happy cry of the calisthenickers;*

*Then those nautical noises that Masefield finds fetching—*
*Knees creaking, and rubber stretching,*

As the Early Birdies reach for their toes,
Which they've not even seen since when, God knows.

* * *

Why can't they just bring you crackers and broth
And leave you to snooze like a three-toed sloth?
You've paid your way on this thousand-dollar ship,
You're not here on an athletic scholarship;
Besides, the girls who infest these tournaments
Are usually not their sex's ornaments.*

**THE COACH**

The erudite George (Doc) Jacobs, athletic director and basketball coach at Vermont's St. Michael's College, wrote this marvelous parody on a famous Rudyard Kipling poem:

A Coach there was and he made his prayer
(Even as you and I)
To a bat and a ball and years of strife
Only to feel the Critics' knife
But the fool called it his way of life
(Even as you and I)

Oh the years we waste and the tears we waste
And the work of head and hand
Belong to the poor coach who did not know
(And now he knows he will never know)
And cannot understand

A Coach there was and the time he spent
(Even as you and I)
To teach a quarterback with good intent

* From *Everyone But Thee and Me,* by Ogden Nash, © 1958, reprinted by permission of Little, Brown and Company, publishers.

*But the boy called a play that was not meant*
*(Even as you and I)*

*Oh the play we lost and the game we lost*
*Though excellent things were planned*
*Belongs to the Coach who didn't know why*
*And now we know he will never know why*
*And cannot understand,*

*The Coach was stripped of all his pride*
*(Even as you and I)*
*When the fans of the team threw him aside*
*Though some of him lived, most of him died*
*(Even as you and I)*

*Oh, why can't the game ever be won*
*With a last minute hit or a goal*
*And it isn't the blame and it isn't the shame*
*That stings the coach like a red-hot coal*
*It's coming to know he will never know*
*And never will understand.*

**PICKING THE WINNERS**

Dismayed at seeing so many of his oldest friends passing on, Grantland Rice wrote this moving piece of verse, addressed to Charon, the mythical Boatman of the Styx:

*The Flame of the Inn is dim tonight—*
*Too many vacant chairs—*
*The sun has lost too much of its light—*
*Too many songs have taken flight—*
*Too many ghosts on the stairs—*
*Charon—here's to you—as man to man—*
*I wish I could pick 'em the way you can.*

**FAMOUS LAST WORDS**

"What's this about putting the quarterback right up against the center? Are you some kind of a nut, Mr. Shaughnessy?"

"You'll never make the team if you keep shooting with one hand, Luisetti."

*"I've got a crazy kid named O'Brien who thinks he can shot-put with his back turned toward the center of the circle."*

"He's much too skinny to be allowed to play with those older boys, Mrs. Chamberlain."

*"Stick to chemistry and you'll be making $10,000 a year by the time you're forty. What kind of future is there in football coaching, Knute?"*

"Your son turned down a scholarship to Oklahoma? What's to become of poor Roger now, Mrs. Maris?"

"*Look here, Musial, you're crazy to quit pitching and switch to the outfield.*"

"Want a laugh? I've got a nutty kid named Arizin who jumps off the floor before he shoots!"

"*Poor Mrs. Arcaro. It's going to be tough raising a kid who's practically a midget.*"

"You're crazy to give up a $15,000 pro football contract, Whizzer. You'll be just another lawyer."

"*Keep going for homers and you'll be waived right out of the league, Babe.*"

"You must be out of your mind, Alonzo. You can't *throw* a football!"

"*Study a little harder and cut out all that running and jumping around, or you'll never amount to anything, Jesse.*"

"You're going to hurt yourself if you keep sliding into bases, Ty."

"*Giving up your newspaper route to become a boxer? You're making a terrible mistake, Rocky.*"

"If you don't tell your boy Willie to stop hanging around pool rooms, you're going to wind up with a bum on your hands, Mrs. Mosconi."

"*A game that has eighteen players, four bases, nine*

innings, four balls, three strikes, a horsehide ball, and needs six acres of ground? It'll never go, Mr. Doubleday."

"With his terrible temper, William can never hope to become a good tennis player, Mr. Tilden."

"Someday you'll be seeing players 6–2, and maybe even taller, running, shooting, and passing just like the little men—sure as my name is James Naismith."

"That bad leg of yours is very dangerous. As your doctor, I strongly suggest that you take up a sedentary occupation, Mickey."

"All right, so you can kick a football pretty good. But better brush up on your blocking and tackling or you'll never make it in college, Groza."

"He's a nice, sweet, little colt, and I'm thinking of giving him to my nephew as a pet. Just for laughs we've named him Man-O-War."

"Keep fooling around with that trick stuff and see how far it gets you, Cousy."

## WHAT DID YOU DO TO RONALD?*

By Michael Green
In the London Observer

* Reprinted by courtesy of *The Observer*, London.

*The Secretary*
*Old Rottinghamians R.F.C.*
*Power Station Lane, Rottingham*

*Dear Sir:*

What have you done to my son?

Ronald left home after a light lunch yesterday to play Rugby with your club for the first time. Although I myself have never played Rugby, I gave my blessing to the idea because Ronald is a shy, delicate lad who has never belonged to any clubs or sporting bodies except the local philatelic society, and we felt the experience would draw him out.

I have read many speeches by leading officials of the Rugby Union, and from these I gather that it is supposed to be a splendid game for developing a sound physique and a good character. In short, we hoped it would make a man of Ronald. When he left home, he was sober, in his right mind and well-dressed.

Imagine my feelings when a shambling, mumbling derelict was deposited outside my front door at midnight.

I was aroused from bed by a prolonged ringing of the front-door bell, and on opening the door I beheld my son leaning with his elbow on the bellpush while two dim figures could be discerned scurrying round the corner. At first I could not recognize Ronald. His mouth was severely contused and there was a mass of dried blood on his left ear. Someone had apparently rowelled his cheek with a set of nails. The end of his tie had been cut off. Worst of all, he reeked of stale beer fumes and was able to talk only in a mumble.

At the sight of me he burst into laughter and started to bawl some verse about the daughter of a character called O'Reilly, which contained words of such a disgusting nature that I was obliged to place my hand over his bruised and battered mouth to prevent his mother overhearing them.

Ronald was removed to bed and undressed, being incapable of doing this himself. Someone called "Taffy" had written his name across Ronald's back with a red ball-point pen. The inscription would not wash out, despite the application of detergent, and I presume it will have to stay until it wears off.

Ronald was too ill to get up in the morning, but in the afternoon I questioned him about what had happened and was unable to gain any clear explanation, except that as it was the first proper match of the season there had been some sort of celebration. His mother told me that there was a large lipstick stain on his collar. He could not account for this.

I can only hazard a guess at what went on. I demand, sir, an account of what happens at your club. Otherwise, I shall place a copy of this letter in the hands of the President of the Rugby Union and the Chief Constable.

Believe me, I am not a spoilsport. When younger I frequently induged in good-humoured bonhomie after an exhilarating hike, but this is too much.

*Yours faithfully,*
R. FOSTER

*R. Foster Esq.*
*Hillside*
*Wordsworth Drive, Rottingham*

*Dear Mr. Foster:*

It was jolly decent of you to write and I'm sorry you were so upset. Actually we were a bit worried ourselves. You see the Rugby Union is trying to urge everyone to start up Colts' sides this season because so many youngsters are coming into the game and we thought we ought to start one, and Ronald, of course, should have played in the Colts, but only three blokes turned up. (I told the committee we could never do it, but they wouldn't listen.)

Well, the Extra B were seven short, so we put the Colts in the Extra B and I'm afraid they were playing some old enemies of ours who have a lot of oldstagers in the side (Welsh, you know) and the match was a little rough. Actually, Ronald hurt his ear during half-time when someone kicked the ball to him and he wasn't looking. As regards his cheek, I believe somebody trod on his face. Don't worry, we know who it was and will be looking for him next time we play them.

Well, being the first night of the season we had a little "do" in the new pavilion and I'm afraid that during this Ronald put his foot through the plate glass window at the front and broke it. I'm told this will cost about 30 pounds to replace and we aren't insured, so I'm wondering if you could see your way to do something about it.

While on the subject, we are still short of some 2,000 pounds to pay for the pavilion and as you are so obviously interested in sport I wonder if you had thought of becoming a life member of our club.

It costs only ten guineas and this entitles you to see every match for nothing and to use the bar whenever you want. (Officially we shut at ten-thirty but you can usually get something up to midnight if you go in through the little door by the visitors' changing-room.) We have a flourishing darts team, a football swindle and an annual sweep on the St. Leger. Last year one of our players was reserve for a County trial match, so we hope that at last the old club is on the up-and-up.

I look forward to hearing from you.

*Yours sincerely,*
A. BROWN, *Secretary, Old Rotts. R.F.C.*

P.S. We are starting Bingo sessions in the clubhouse every Thursday, beginning next week. Ladies welcome.

## WHAT IS AN OFFICIAL?

*By Peter Billick*
*Rochester, N. Y.*

Between the exuberance of the winner and the downhearted dismay of the loser, we find a creature called an official. Officials come in assorted sizes and shapes, but usually are dressed in the same type of uniform. All, however, have the same creed: to watch every play of every quarter of every game and to call the plays to the best of their ability as they see them.

Officials are found everywhere—on the field, in the gym, on the track, on the diamond, in the pool—on top of, running around, jumping over, climbing through, and always with whistle ready, looking, looking, looking for some infraction.

Fellow officials rib them, athletes tolerate them, spectators boo them, coaches criticize them, wives adore them, sons and daughters idolize them, and mothers worry about them.

An official is Courage in cleats, Spirit in stripes, Wisdom with a whistle. Despite the fact they get paid for their work, they have a devotion to duty above and beyond their obligation to their employer.

When the game is close, the officials are incompetent, indecisive, and stupid. When it is one-sided, they are merciless, whistle-happy, careless, and domineering.

An official is a composite. He looks like a gentleman, acts like a traffic cop, is as fussy as an old grandmother with her sewing basket, as immaculate as a debutante, and as big a ham as Elvis Presley playing Hamlet in Madison Square Garden.

To himself, an official has never missed a play, called a ball a strike, or split a second incorrectly with a stopwatch. He has the eyes of an eagle, the keen mind of an Einstein, the judgment of a Solomon, and the speed and grace of Joe DiMaggio and Jesse Owens rolled into one.

To the men who work with him, he is always out of position, runs like a truck, steals calls from under his partner's nose, is blind as a bat, stupid as a mule, and is utterly incapable of making a correct decision on anything except who should drive the car.

An official likes trips out of town (with mileage), few training sessions, well-coached teams, considerate coaches, polite players, dry fields, cool, crisp days, and the quiet satisfaction of having been a part of a perfect day. He cares not for wet games, tough decisions, screaming coaches, and irate fans.

An official is a wonderful creature. You can criticize him, but you can't intimidate him. You can question his judgment, but not his honesty. He is the symbol of fair play, integrity, and sportsmanship. He is a hard-working, alert, determined individual who is making a great contribution to the American way of life through athletics.

OTHER BOOKS BY THE AUTHOR

*Treasury of Sports Humor* (1960)

*The Best of Basketball from Scholastic Coach* (1962)

# Index